QUILTING
IN
SQUARES

QUILTING IN SQUARES

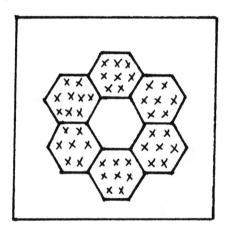

Katharine Fisher
and Elizabeth Kay

Illustrated with Diagrams

CHARLES SCRIBNER'S SONS
NEW YORK

We would like to thank our friends and students who
were kind enough to lend us some of the squares and
quilts appearing in this book:
*Lois Harman, B. L. Buck, Nancy Ryan,
Susan Luchetti, and Betty Dominick.*

New Canaan Quilters:

*Ann Akitt, Jan Moller, Ann Price, Ellen Warden,
Mary Wagner, Val Erichs, Carolyn Scott, Beth Bodnar,
Wendy Stone, Ann Hummel, Nancy Rodts, Carol
Kohler, Nancy Longley, Dorie Peck, Margaret Smith,
Janet Johnson, Concie Hershey, Kristin Johnston,
Barbara Kries, Joan Hutchinson, Mary Bartlett, Carole
Clarkson, Ann Thornton, Shannon Weideman,
and Nancy Thompson.*

Pictures: *Robert Fearon*
    David Kay
    Jonathan Kay
Diagrams: *Katharine Fisher*
Color photography: *Russ Kinne*

Library of Congress Cataloging in Publication Data
Fisher, Katharine.
  Quilting in squares.

   1. Quilting.   I. Kay, Elizabeth, joint author.
II. Title.
TT835.F57   746.4'6   77-16137
ISBN 0-684-15501-X (cloth)
ISBN 0-684-17453-7 (paper)

1 3 5 7 9 11 13 15 17 19 Q/P 20 18 16 14 12 10 8 6 4 2

Printed in the United States of America

To Walt and Kit for their patience and encouragement; to Connie, Sarah, and Lowrie for their enthusiasm from afar; and to my mother.

To Andy, David, Jim, and Jonathan, who never tired of taking pictures of quilts, and to Lynn, who assured me it was all possible. What fun we had!

Contents

■▚■▚■▚■▚■▚■▚■

QUILTING
IN
SQUARES

INTRODUCTION

Quilts are a part of our American heritage. Today's quilts will be tomorrow's heirlooms! Be a part of this and have fun in the process. The old quilt-making method involved large frames and many people to complete a quilt. This is not practical for our life-style today. We will show you how to make a quilt by yourself, following the easy diagrams and instructions. This method is quilting in squares; your quilt can be carried around with you like needlepoint or knitting. You can enjoy sewing when you are waiting in carpools, sitting in meetings, or relaxing at home.

We have three traditional quilts to tell you about. The first is patchwork, which is the easiest and shows you tricks you will use in the other two. Next is appliqué, which is fun and creative. Piecework is the third and is very challenging. Further fun will be learning biscuits, "Crazy Patch," and a really quick confidence-builder, the tied quilt.

FACTS AND FABRICS

Make life easy by buying the right fabrics; 100 percent cotton, calico, muslin, gingham, and Dacron and cotton blends are the best. They hold a fold and are not flimsy or slippery.

Yes—you *must* wash, dry, and press your fabrics before using them. Avoid the heartbreak of shrinkage, running colors, and too much sizing (that shiny surface on new material).

Batting is the filler inside the quilt. It comes in various sizes and thicknesses and can be purchased along with your fabric.

HERE ARE THE SQUARES—TAKE YOUR PICK AND BEGIN

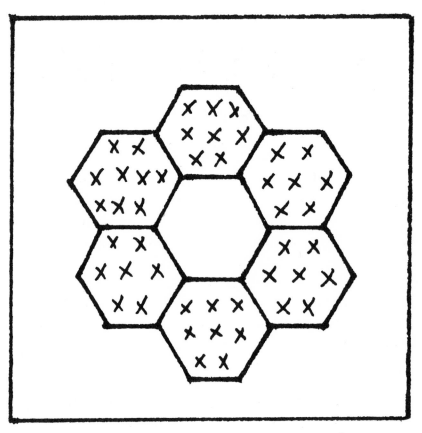

Figure 1   Patchwork

Figure 2

Patchwork

Figure 3

Appliqué

Figure 4

Appliqué

Figure 5

Piecework

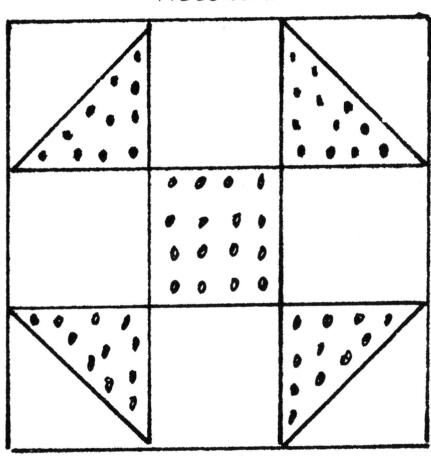

Figure 6

YOU HAVE PICKED A PATTERN—WHAT ABOUT THE SIZE?

Here are *mattress* sizes:

Bassinet	36 inches wide by 36 inches long
Crib	40 inches wide by 60 inches long
Twin	39 inches wide by 72 inches long
Double	54 inches wide by 72 inches long
Queen	60 inches wide by 80 inches long

The size of a quilt is the mattress size plus the overhang (*Figure 7*).

All quilts have top squares and back squares. These may also be referred to as blocks. Top squares may be any size, but 9-inch to 14-inch squares are the easiest to work with.

Quilt edges are usually finished with strips or borders.

We will show you two different ways to make the back of your quilt. In the first you will have the same number of back squares as

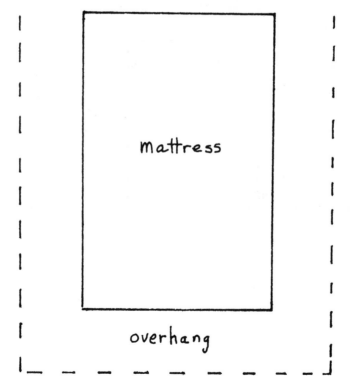

Figure 7

top squares, but the backs will be cut ½ inch larger to make it easier to join the seams later.

In the second method you will cut much larger back squares. These will be the size of four top squares joined together. The larger back square can be used only when there is an *even* number of squares (or blocks) in the quilt. See Plates 1 and 2.

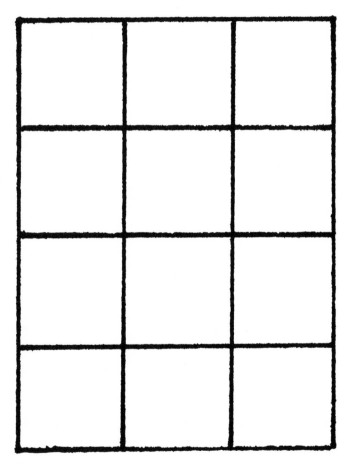

Figure 8

Figure 8 shows a quilt made up of *odd* numbers of top squares in the width and the same number of back squares.

Figure 9 shows a quilt made up of an *even* number of top squares using the larger back squares.

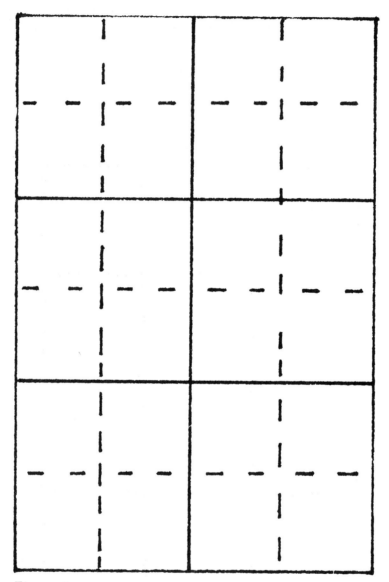

Figure 9

Quilts are not bedspreads. If you are planning a bedspread you must allow for a pillow tuck. This is done by making the quilt longer.

You have picked the type of quilt you are going to make. You have decided how you will make the back of the quilt. You must now decide whether you will finish the edges with strips or with borders. Strips are easy and are what we recommend for a first quilt. Borders are wider, need batting, and must be quilted. If you are planning borders you should use the cutting guide for borders shown on page 24.

IF ARITHMETIC TURNS YOU OFF—here are some charts to help you see how many squares you'll need for the quilt top and back, and the amount of fabric you will need to buy *(Figures 10, 11, 12).*

Measurement Chart

	Over-hang	Square Size	Top Squares Needed	Back Squares Needed	If Using Large Back Squares	Final Quilt Measurement
Bassinet 36″ x 36″	None	9″ x 9″	4 across 4 down	4 across 4 down	2—18″ x 18″	36″ x 36″
Crib 40″ x 60″	None	10″ x 10″	4 across 6 down	4 across 6 down	6—20″ x 20″	40″ x 60″
Twin 39″ x 72″	13″	13″ x 13″	4 across 6 down	4 across 6 down	6—26″ x 26″	52″ x 78″
Double 54″ x 72″	9″	12″ x 12″	6 across 8 down	6 across 8 down	12—24″ x 24″	72″ x 96″
Queen 60″ x 80″	10″	13″ x 13″	6 across 8 down	6 across 8 down	12—26″ x 26″	78″ x 104″

Figure 10

Fabric for Patchwork or Appliqué Patterns

Roughly estimate the amount of fabric used in each square, keeping in mind the number of squares in the quilt. Don't forget to use your scrap bag!

Fabric Chart for Quilts
For Top and Back Only

	For the Top	*For the Back*
Bassinet	1¼ yards	1¼ yards
Crib	2 yards	2 yards
Twin	4 yards	4 yards
Double	5½ yards	5½ yards
Queen	6 yards	6 yards

Figure 11

Bedspreads—Squares and Fabric Needed

	Top	Back	*If Using Large Back* Squares	*Fabric Needed* Top	Back
Twin	4 across 8 down	4 across 8 down	2 across 4 down	5½ yards	5½ yards
Double	6 across 8 down	6 across 8 down	3 across 4 down	6 yards	6 yards
Queen	6 across 10 down	6 across 10 down	3 across 5 down	8 yards	8 yards

Figure 12

Fabric for a Pieced Top

Look at one square. Determine roughly what proportion of each color is in that square. Example: ½ blue, ¼ white, ¼ yellow. If your total top requires 6 yards of fabric, buy 3 yards (½) blue, 1½ yards (¼) white, and 1½ yards (¼) yellow.

Armed with all the facts and figures, head for a fabric store. Don't forget to buy the batting.

Patchwork and appliqué quilts—cut top and back squares. Piecework quilts—cut only back squares (the tops are made up of pieces of fabric sewn together).

Reach for scissors, ruler, pencil, and pins. You are ready to attack your washed, dried, and pressed fabrics. Cut all the squares, following the easy cutting guide you have chosen.

Cutting Guide Using Small Back Squares

1. Make a cardboard pattern the size of the top square you are using.

2. Make a cardboard pattern ½ inch larger for the back square.

3. Cut the back squares first, using the common lines.

4. Don't cut the shaded area (*Figure 13*); save it for the strips.

5. Cut the batting squares the same size as the top squares.

Cutting Guide Using Large Back Squares

1. Make a cardboard pattern the size of the top square you are using.

2. Using a tape measure, mark a back square the size of four top squares. Use this as a pattern to cut the rest of the back squares. Cut on common lines.

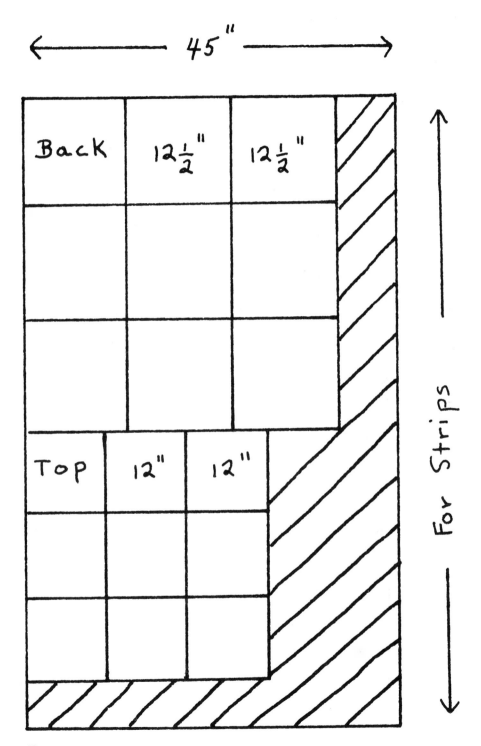

Figure 13

3. Cut the back squares first.

4. Don't cut the shaded area (*Figure 14*); save it for the strips or borders.

5. Cut the batting squares the same size as the large back square.

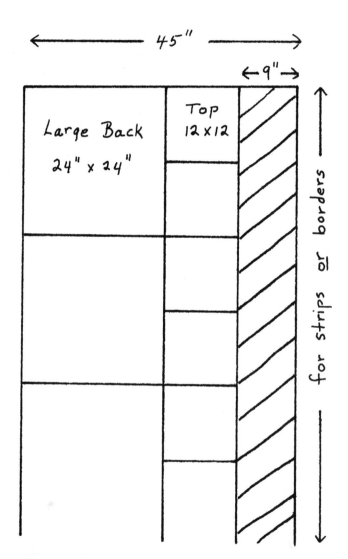

Figure 14

FOR MATH MAJORS

How to Determine Measurements

1. Know the mattress size of the bed.

2. Decide how much the quilt will hang over the sides of the bed (*Figure 7*).

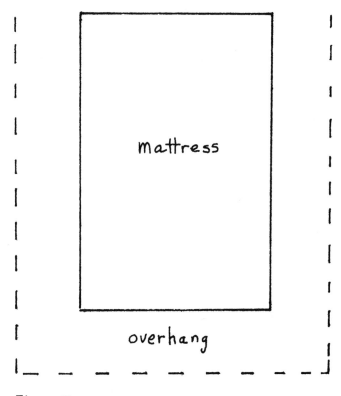

Figure 7

3. Determine the actual size of the quilt, using the formula below:

OVERHANG + MATTRESS WIDTH + OVERHANG =
QUILT *WIDTH*.
MATTRESS LENGTH + OVERHANG = QUILT *LENGTH*.

4. *For the quilt top*: Decide on the size square (block) that best fits into the measurements. (This may change the overall quilt size by a few inches.) First divide the square size into the width measurement. This gives you the number of squares going *across* the quilt. Then divide the square size into the length measurement to determine the number of squares in the quilt's *length*. Multiply the two together to find out the total number of squares in the quilt top.

For the quilt back: If you are using *small* back squares you will need the same number of squares as the top but they must be ½ inch larger.

For large back squares: Divide the number of top squares by 4 and this gives you the number you need.

5. Write down the quilt measurements. Write down the number of top squares and the number of back squares you will need. With these numbers figure out the yards of fabric you will need to buy.

FIGURE THE FABRIC

If Your Quilt Has Small Top and Back Squares

Using the number of squares in the quilt back, figure out how many squares will fit across the *width* of 45-inch fabric. Divide this number into the total number of squares in the quilt back. This tells you how many *rows* of squares you will need going down the *length* of the fabric. Now take this same number of rows and multiply it by the size of your square. This will give you the number of inches you need for the *back*. Convert this to yards.

For the top squares: Proceed exactly the same way. Then add the yardage for the top and back together, and ½ YARD EXTRA FOR GOOD MEASURE! Check *Figure 15* for converting inches to yards.

Cut the squares, using the cutting guide for small back squares in *Figure 13*.

If Your Quilt Has Large Back Squares

For the Back Squares

Take the number of large back squares you need and figure out how many will fit across 45-inch fabric (it is usually only one). Divide this number into the total number of large squares in the quilt back. This tells you how many *rows* of squares you will need going down the *length* of the fabric. Now take this same number of rows and multiply it by the size of your large square. This will give you the number of inches you need for the back squares. Convert this to yards.

HELPFUL CHART FOR CONVERTING INCHES TO YARDS

36 inches	=	1	yard
72 ″	=	2	yards
108 ″	=	3	″
144 ″	=	4	″
180 ″	=	5	″
216 ″	=	6	″
252 ″	=	7	″
288 ″	=	8	″
324 ″	=	9	″
360 ″	= 10		″
396 ″	= 11		″
432 ″	= 12		″

Figure 15

For the Top Squares

You can see from *Figure 14* that there is room for two top squares beside each large back square. This will take care of half the total number of top squares you need. Figure out how many of the remaining top squares will fit across 45-inch fabric. Divide this number into the top squares still needed. This tells you how many *rows* of squares you'll need going down the *length* of the fabric. Now take this same number of rows and multiply it by the size of your square. This will give you the number of inches needed for the rest of the top squares. Convert to yards and add all the yardage together, plus ½ YARD EXTRA FOR GOOD MEASURE! Check *Figure 15* for converting inches to yards.

Cut the squares, using the cutting guide for large back squares in *Figure 14*.

This is the cutting guide we suggest you use if your are planning borders. Nine-inch borders can be cut from the shaded area.

BE A NEAT-NIC

Collect the supplies and materials you need.

Quilting thread comes in white and colors. It is waxed so it will slide through the three layers easily. It also doesn't tangle, so use it for all sewing.

Batting comes in sizes from crib to queen (for king you need two twin packages). It also comes in various thicknesses. Avoid "super fluff" unless you are making a tied quilt.

A word to the wise: quilt all the blocks in the same color so the back of the quilt looks as lovely as the front. Quilting needles are short and sharp. Use these or regular sewing needles.

Stop, pause, and *think*—then cut the squares and patterns.

Stuff everything needed for each square in a plastic bag and carry it around with you. Friends will wonder if you are pulling out a sandwich or your sewing!

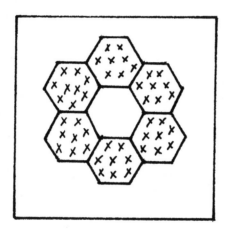

1
PATCHWORK

First Things First—
A HEXAGON SQUARE IS THE EASIEST TO LEARN

"Grandmother's Flower Garden," which is made up of hexagons, was a very popular quilt pattern in this country. Paper liners were used to aid in the construction. Often these paper liners were left sewn in the quilts to provide added warmth; they are also one of the ways by which we have been able to date antique quilts.

29

This is one 12-inch x 12-inch hexagon square (*Figure 16*). Let's make it!

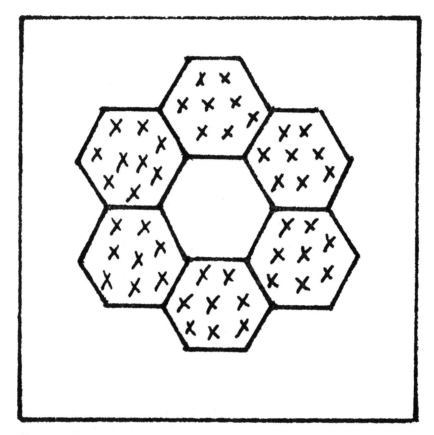

Figure 16

Trace the hexagon (*Figure 17*) very accurately onto tracing paper. Transfer it to shirt cardboard, using a ruler and carbon paper. Cut the cardboard hexagon out on the line. This is a pattern, called a template. In order to make accurate fabric hexagons you need to cut paper liners. To do this place the cardboard hexagon template on top of not more than two thicknesses of magazine paper. Draw

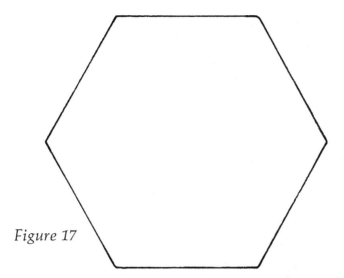

Figure 17

around the template and cut on the line. Six paper liners make up a circle of hexagons (seven if you would like a hexagon in the center). Set the paper liners aside and take out the pretty prints you are using for the hexagons (you may want to use a plain color, too).

Place the cardboard template on the *wrong* side of the fabric on the straight of the goods. Hexagon *A* (*Figure 18*) is placed correctly with two of its sides running with the straight; *B* is incorrect.

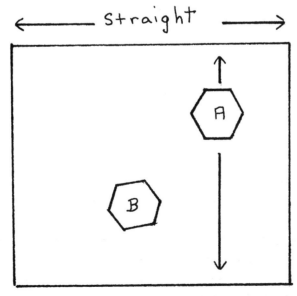

Figure 18

Draw around the template with a pencil. Then draw five more hexagons, allowing ¼-inch seam allowance around each. Cut each hexagon out, cutting ¼-inch seam allowance by eye (*Figure 19*). (The line will scream at you to cut on it, but don't! Cut ¼ inch away from it.)

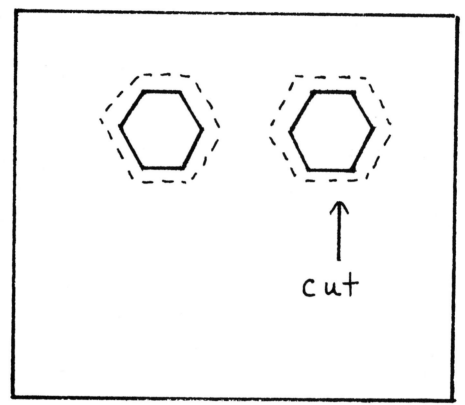

Figure 19

Pin a paper liner on the wrong side of each fabric hexagon. Fold fabric edges over and baste down into the paper, neatly folding the corners over (*Figure 20*).

Join the hexagons as follows: Pin two hexagons right sides together. Using matching single thread, hide the knot in the fold. Sew as in *Figure 21*, catching each edge with small stitches. This stitch is called the whipping stitch. Join three hexagons together first, then

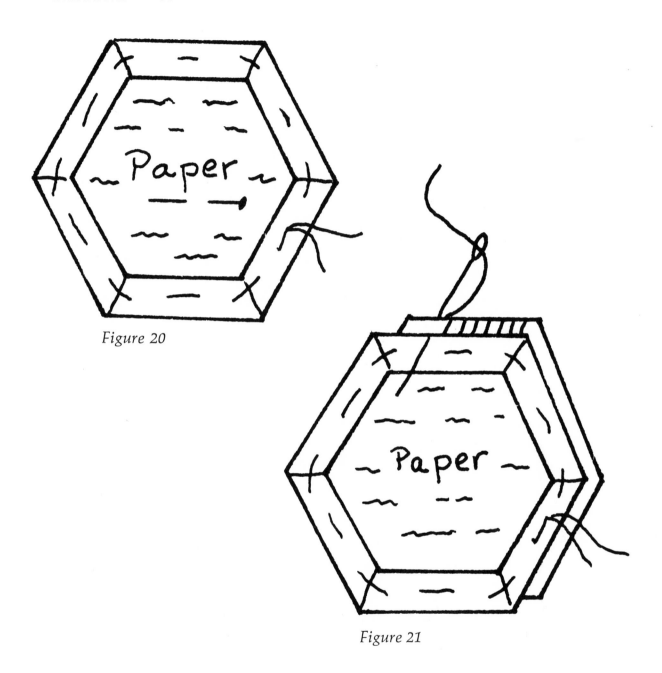

Figure 20

Figure 21

join the other three. Now join the two sections, using the same whipping stitch (*Figure 22*). Press the hexagon circle, papers and all. The time to remove the papers and bastings is now (unless this quilt is for your unheated cottage!).

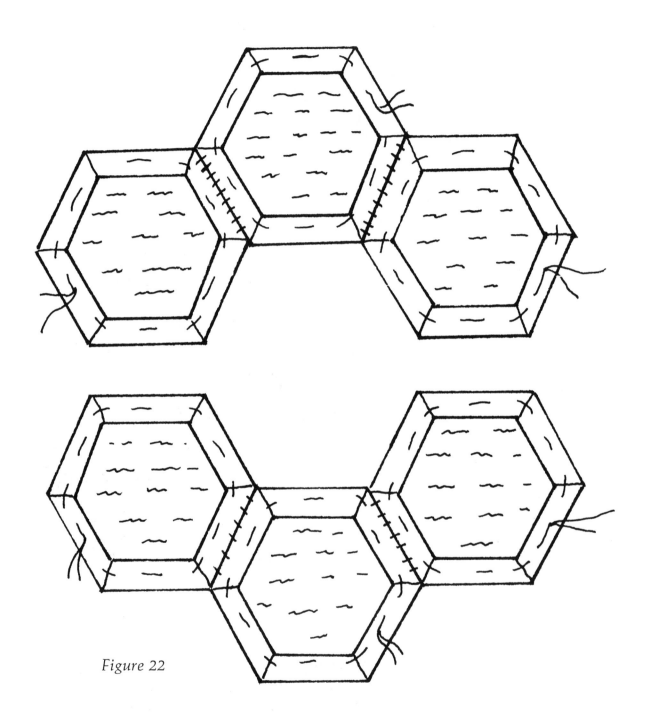

Figure 22

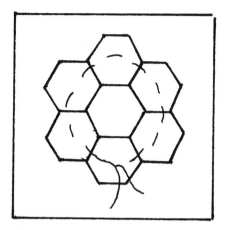

Figure 23

Pin and baste the hexagon circle to the center of a top square (*Figure 23*). Stitch it down as follows: Knot the thread and come up from underneath into the fold. Go down directly opposite where you came up originally. Continue going forward; the stitches are about ¼ inch apart. The stitches on the right side will not show if your up-and-down stitches are directly opposite each other (*Figure 24*). This stitch is called the blind stitch. It is used to anchor the patchwork to a piece of fabric, in this case the top square. When you are finished sewing, give it a good press, step back, and take a look —aren't you pleased?

Figure 24

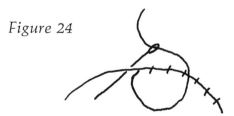

Blind Stitch

IT'S QUILTING TIME!

The purpose of quilting is to hold the three layers together: the top, the batting, and the back (the back square is the underside of a quilt block, sometimes called the "backing" square). The three layers are put together like a sandwich.

Place the backing square on a table wrong side up, and lay the batting square on top of it. Then put the hexagon square on top of both, right side up. Pin the three layers together and baste from the center out, having the knots on the top for easy removal (*Figure 25*).

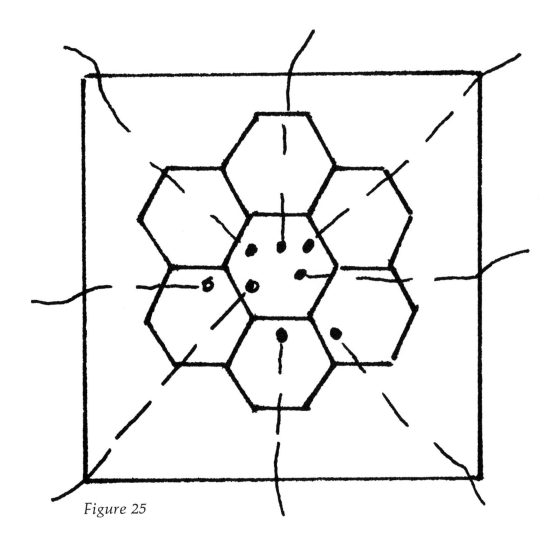

Figure 25

How to Quilt

The quilting stitch is a small running stitch going down through all three layers: the top, the batting, and the backing. It is evenly spaced and evenly stitched. Generally you should have five to seven stitches to the inch, but don't get into a panic if they don't

Figure 26

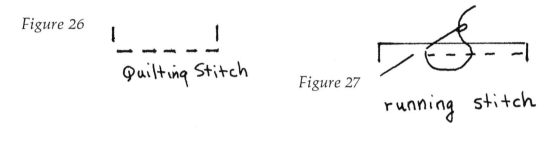

Figure 27

Figure 28a

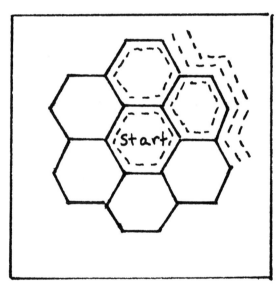

measure up. Go for even stitches, not the tiny, tiny ones (*Figures 26, 27*).

Thread a needle with a single piece of quilting thread. Make a *small* knot, snip off the tail, and put your thimble on the third finger of your hand. Start by coming up from underneath at the center-most point (*Figure 28a*). Give a quick pull, losing the knot in the batting—it makes a clicking sound. (Pulling the backing square away makes it easier for the knot to slip through.) Go straight down through all three layers, touching your finger, and then come up to the top, making a small stitch. (Touching your finger ensures that you have gone through the three layers.) Take two, three, or four stitches on the needle and then draw through. Never mind if your finger gets sore—it will develop a callus very quickly and the fun and beauty of quilting far surpasses a slightly worn-looking finger!

To end the thread off, go down to the underside of the backing square and take a stitch, going through the backing square and catching some batting. Then take another stitch right over the previous stitch. Now run the needle off to the side through the batting, pull the fabric up a little, and snip off the thread. The end is lost between the layers.

The amount of quilting you do is a matter of personal preference. It is most important to quilt from the center of the square toward the edges. This prevents the batting from bunching up in the center. The stitches will become even with practice. Don't pull them too tightly; let them flow. A very important point to remember: don't quilt any closer to the edge of the square than a good ½ inch. You will need the ½ inch of unquilted fabric when you join the square to another square as you put the quilt together. (More than ½ inch of unquilted fabric around the edge makes the whole process even easier!)

You have made "Grandmother's Square." Turn it over—the back is beautiful *(Figure 28b)*!

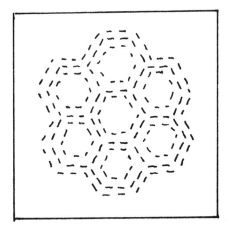

Figure 28 b

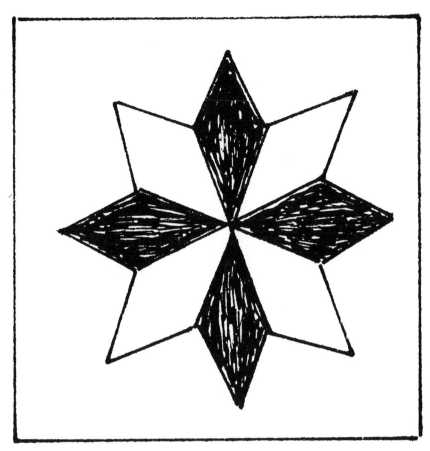

Figure 29

ANOTHER PATCHWORK PATTERN—MAYBE DIAMONDS ARE FOR YOU!

Star quilts lead the list of American patterns. "Twinkling Star," "Shooting Star," "Star of Bethlehem," and "Texas Star" are some of the many names given these gorgeous quilts. They are made exactly like the hexagon quilts but the pattern is a diamond.

Let's make a diamond square. It's very much the same as a circle of hexagons. All the steps are the same except for making the diamond. Follow the easy diagrams. This is one 12-inch x 12-inch diamond square (*Figure 29*). Look at it and plan your fabrics.

Accuracy is most important! Trace the diamond in *Figure 30*. Make a cardboard template and eight paper liners (eight diamonds make up a circle).

Place the cardboard template on the *wrong* side of the fabric so that two sides of the diamond are on the straight of the goods. Diamond *A* (*Figure 31*) is placed correctly with two sides running with the straight; *B* is incorrect. Cut the ¼-inch seam allowance by eye—remember, *not* on the line (*Figure 32*)!

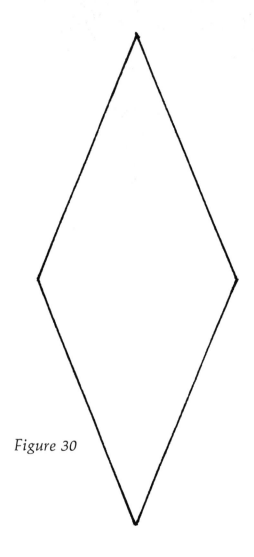

Figure 30

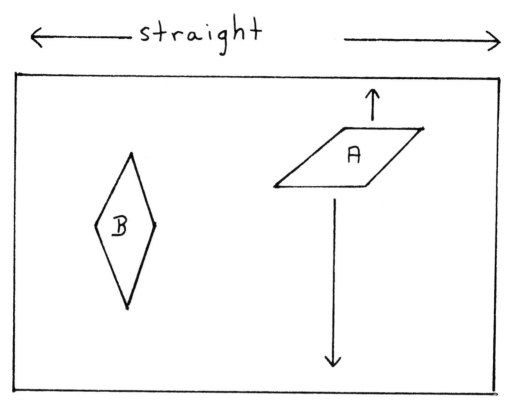

Figure 31

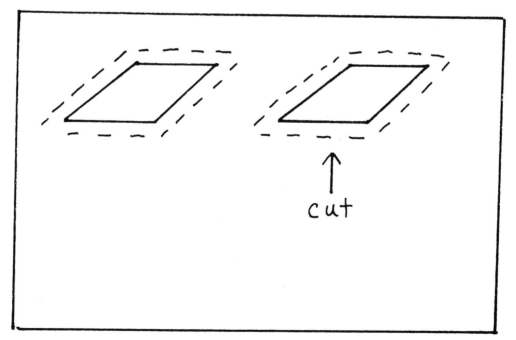

Figure 32

Pin the paper liners to the wrong side of the diamonds and fold the edges over. Points *A* and *B* are folded the same way as the hexagons. Points *C* and *D* are folded differently in order to make sharp points. Knowing how to make these sharp points is one of the tricks in sewing. Fold the fabric over point *C*, and then fold each side in and baste around the edges (*Figures 33, 34*).

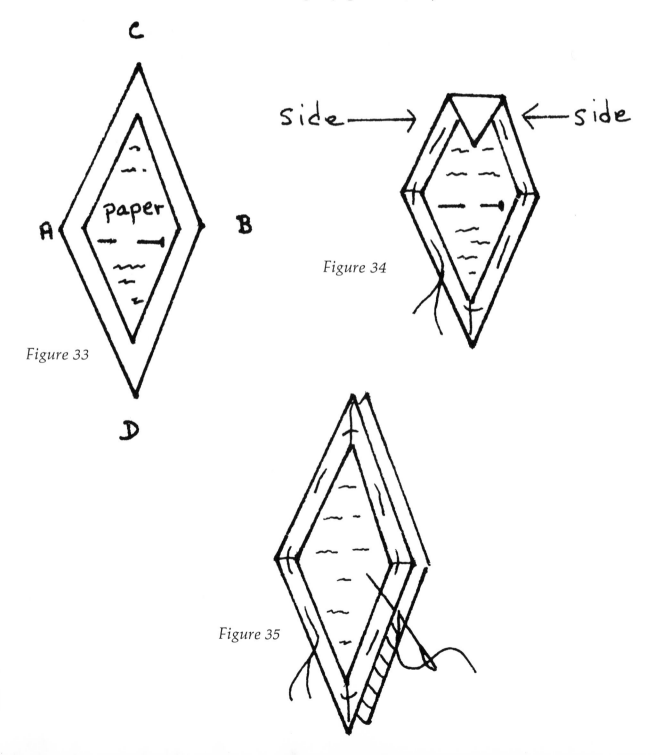

Figure 33

Figure 34

Figure 35

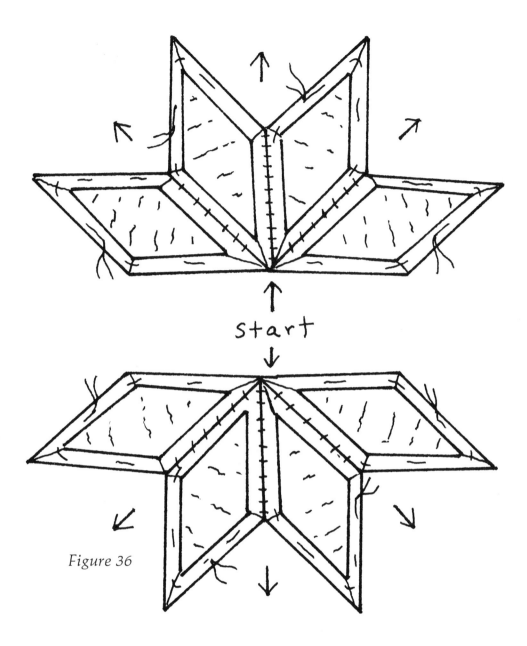

Figure 36

Join the diamonds, using the whipping stitch. Whip four diamonds together first, then the other four, and then join both sections. Start at the point that will be the center of the star (*Figures 35, 36*).

Press the finished star of diamonds and remove the papers and bastings.

Center the star on a top square; pin and baste it down.

When the blind stitching is finished, give the square a good press. Quilt it the same way as the hexagon and see how pretty it looks (*Figure 37*).

"Twinkling Star," "Morning Star," "Shooting Star," and yours—the "Square Star"! Learn to put all those star blocks together by turning to Chapter 4, "Building Blocks into Quilts."

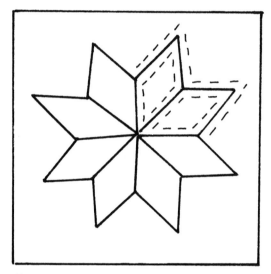

Figure 37

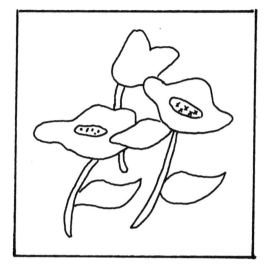

2
APPLIQUÉ

W"reath of Roses," "Basket of Flowers," pineapples, tulips, trees, "Sunbonnet Sue," "Buffalo Bill," "Spot the Dog," and the "Calico Cat"—all and anything lends itself to appliqué. Perhaps the marriage quilts are the most famous of the traditional patterns. A bride-to-be was given squares made by her family and friends. Each square was an appliquéd picture symbolic of life. Almost always a heart was found somewhere on the quilt. You don't necessarily have to be an artist to do appliqué. Patterns can be found in books and catalogs. A child's coloring book with simple line drawings is a wonderful source of patterns. Whether you use a ready-made pattern or create one, it will be all yours because of the fabric *you* have picked to use. See Plates 21 and 22.

"SUNBONNET SUE"

Figure 38

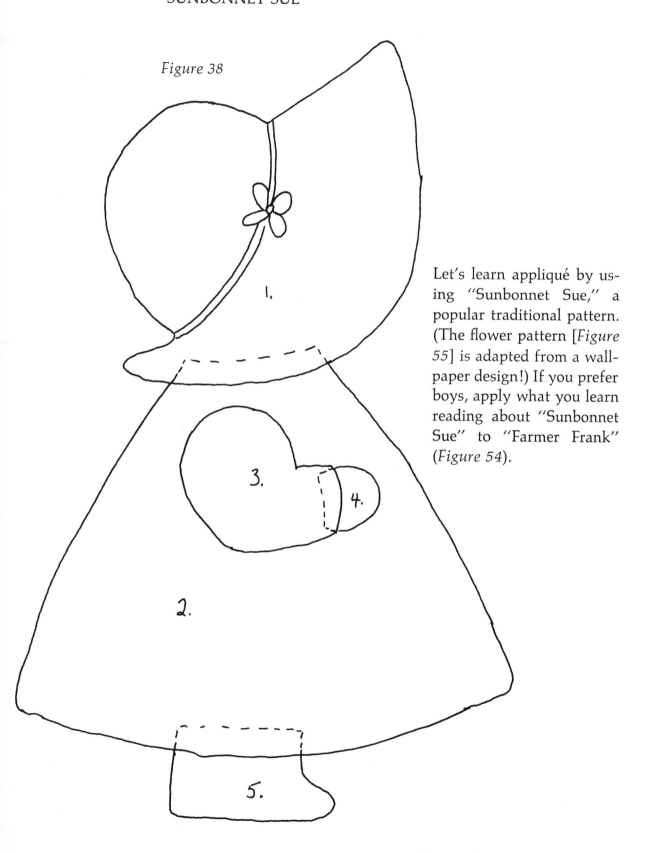

Let's learn appliqué by using "Sunbonnet Sue," a popular traditional pattern. (The flower pattern [*Figure 55*] is adapted from a wallpaper design!) If you prefer boys, apply what you learn reading about "Sunbonnet Sue" to "Farmer Frank" (*Figure 54*).

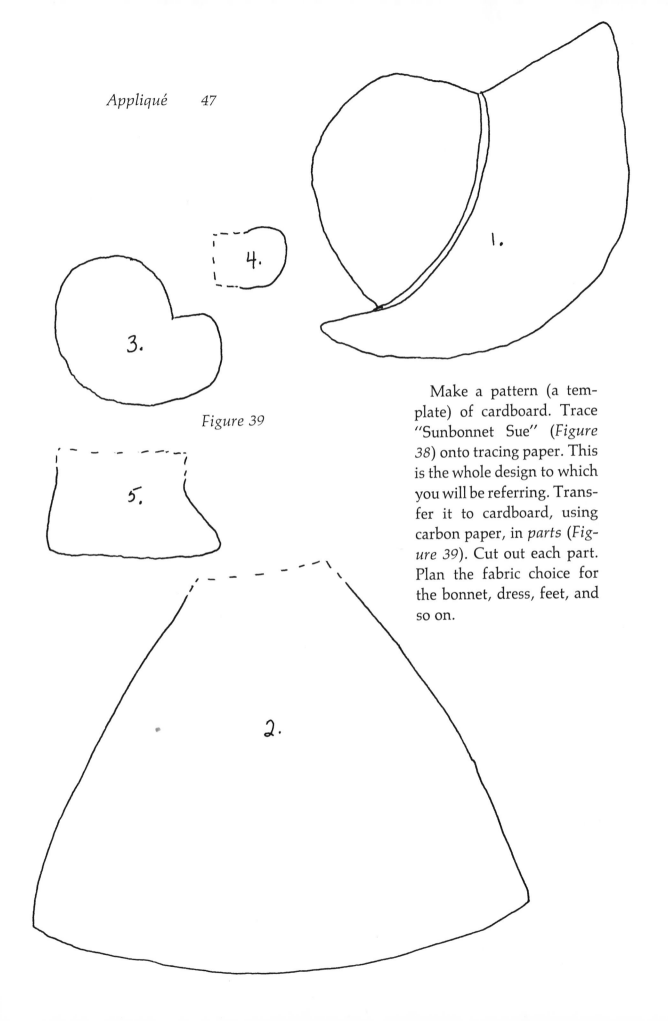

Figure 39

Make a pattern (a template) of cardboard. Trace "Sunbonnet Sue" (*Figure 38*) onto tracing paper. This is the whole design to which you will be referring. Transfer it to cardboard, using carbon paper, in *parts* (*Figure 39*). Cut out each part. Plan the fabric choice for the bonnet, dress, feet, and so on.

Place the template parts on the *right* side of the fabric, not too close together, and mark with a pencil just dark enough to see. Cut the parts out, leaving ¼-inch seam allowance by eye around each section. Extend the parts that go under—for example, the hand has to fit under the dress sleeve, the shoes under the dress (*Figure 40*).

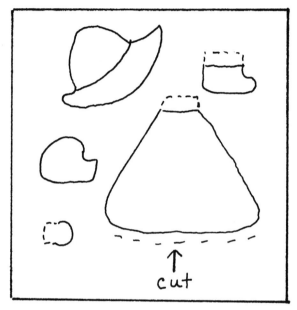

Figure 40

In order to make the appliqué lie flat you must clip the curves and V's. Snip to the seam line (*Figure 41*).

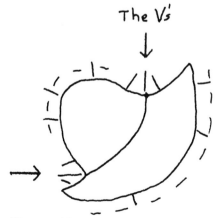

Figure 41

Here is a trick to help you make sharp points on the bonnet (use it in future sewing projects!):

1. Fold point *A* over.

2. Then fold each side in (*Figures 42, 43, 44*).

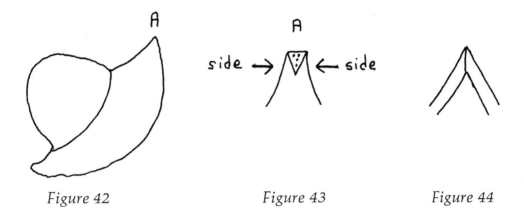

Figure 42   Figure 43   Figure 44

Set Her on Top

Pin or baste "Sunbonnet Sue" in place on a top square, referring to the original drawing (*Figure 45*).

Figure 45

Thread your needle with matching single thread and prepare to sew her down. Turn the edges under on the pencil line. It is not necessary to pin or baste before you sew, as working with the needle and one or two pins is satisfactory. Remember—no need to turn the top of the shoes in, because they fit under the dress.

Blind stitch as follows: Knot the thread and come up from underneath into the fold. Go down directly opposite where you came up originally. Continue going forward; the stitches are about ¼ inch apart. The stitches on the right side will not show if your up-and-down stitches are directly opposite each other. This stitch is used to anchor the appliqué. It is quite invisible (*Figure 46*).

Figure 46

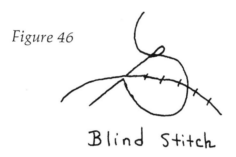

Blind Stitch

Decorate "Sue" with Embroidery

Put a bow on her bonnet, a flower in her hand, or add trim to her dress. Embroidery on appliqué is like icing on a cake. Use two or three strands of embroidery floss.

Stem Stitch (Figure 47)

1. Needle comes up at *a*, down at *b*, up at *c*, which is halfway between *a* and *b*. Draw through, holding thread *either* above or below the needle.

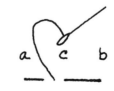

Figure 47a

2. Needle goes down at *d* and up at *b* in the same hole made previously.

Continue going forward, always being sure to hold the thread on the same side of needle (either above or below).

Figure 47 *b*

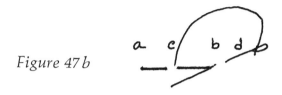

Split Stitch (Figure 48)

Thread comes up at *a*, down at *b*, and up at *c* halfway between *a* and *b* and splits the stitch exactly in the middle.

Figure 48

Arrow Head (Figure 49)

Needle comes up at *a*, down at *b*, up at *c*, down at *a*, up at *d*, and down at *a*. Continue going forward.

"Sunbonnet Sue" is finished—just iron out her wrinkles.

Figure 49

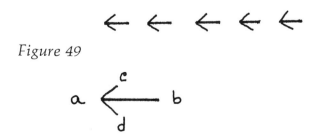

START QUILTING

The purpose of quilting is to hold the three layers together: the top, the batting, and the back (the back square is the underside of a quilt block, sometimes called the "backing square"). Stack, then baste the layers—the backing, batting, and top square—together like a sandwich.

Baste the appliqué square (*Figure 50*).

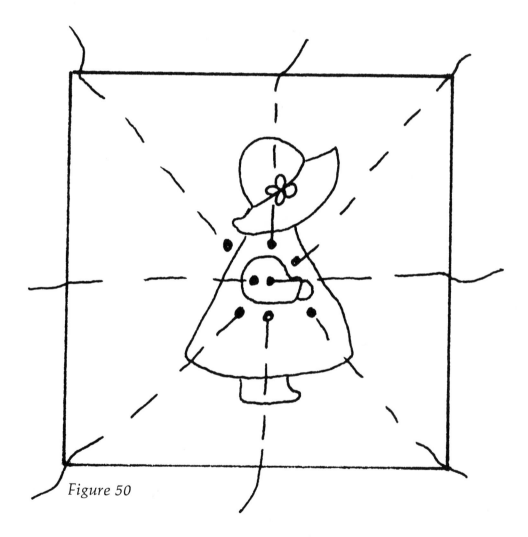

Figure 50

How to Quilt

The quilting stitch is a small running stitch going down through all three layers: the top, the batting, and the backing. It is evenly spaced and evenly stitched (*Figures 51, 52*). Generally you should have five to seven stitches to the inch, but don't worry if you don't—you should improve with practice.

Figure 51

running stitch

Figure 52

quilting stitch

Thread a needle with a single piece of quilting thread. Make a small knot, snip off the tail, and put your thimble on the third finger of your hand. Start by coming up from underneath at the center-most point (*Figure 53*). Give a quick pull, losing the knot in the bat-ting—it makes a clicking sound. (This may take some practice. Pull-ing the backing square away makes it easier for the knot to slip through.) Go straight through all three layers, touching your finger, and then come up to the top, making a small stitch. (Touching your finger ensures that you have gone through the three layers.) Take

Figure 53

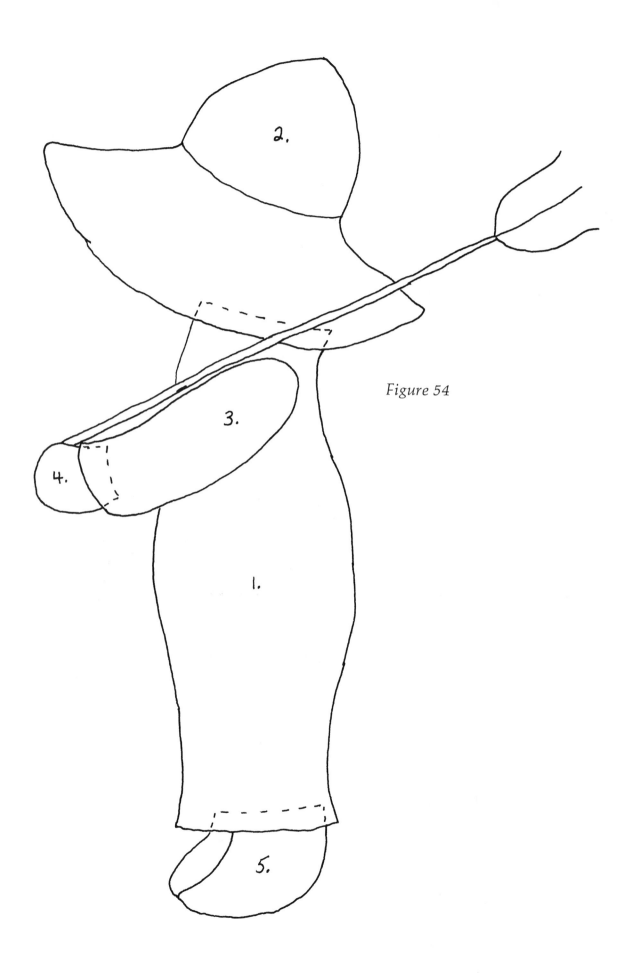

Figure 54

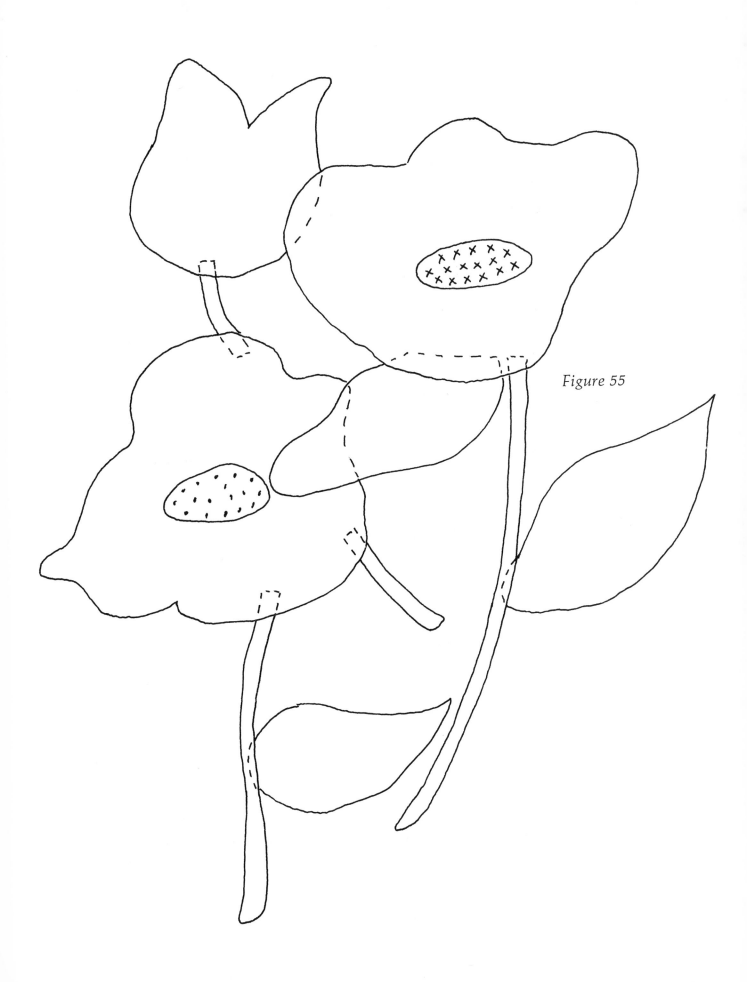

Figure 55

two, three, or four stitches on the needle and then draw through. If your finger gets sore, wrap a piece of adhesive tape around it. This helps!

To end the thread off, go down to the underside of the backing square and take a stitch, going through the backing square and catching some batting. Then take another stitch right over the previous stitch. Now run the needle off to the side through the batting, pull the fabric up a little, and snip the thread off. The end is lost between the layers.

The amount of quilting you do is a matter of personal preference. It is most important to quilt from the center of the square toward the edges. This prevents the batting from bunching up in the center. Don't pull the stitches too tightly; let them flow. A very important point to remember: don't quilt any closer to the edge of the square than a good ½ inch. You will need the ½ inch of unquilted fabric when you join the square to another square when you put the quilt together. (More than ½ inch of unquilted fabric around the edge makes the whole process even easier!)

A square a day—speeds you on your way.

Other patterns for appliqué: *Figures 54, 55* (pages 54 and 55).

QUILTING DESIGNS

Squares can be made up with quilting designs. These designs are quilted in the outline of any appliqué, patchwork, or pieced pattern.

"Sue"—the Quilt Design

Transfer "Sue" to manila paper with the aid of carbon paper. With a ripper or small sharp scissors, poke holes on all the lines ¼ inch or more apart, and on all the intersections (*Figure 56*). Mark a plain top square with a T (to indicate the top of the square). Place

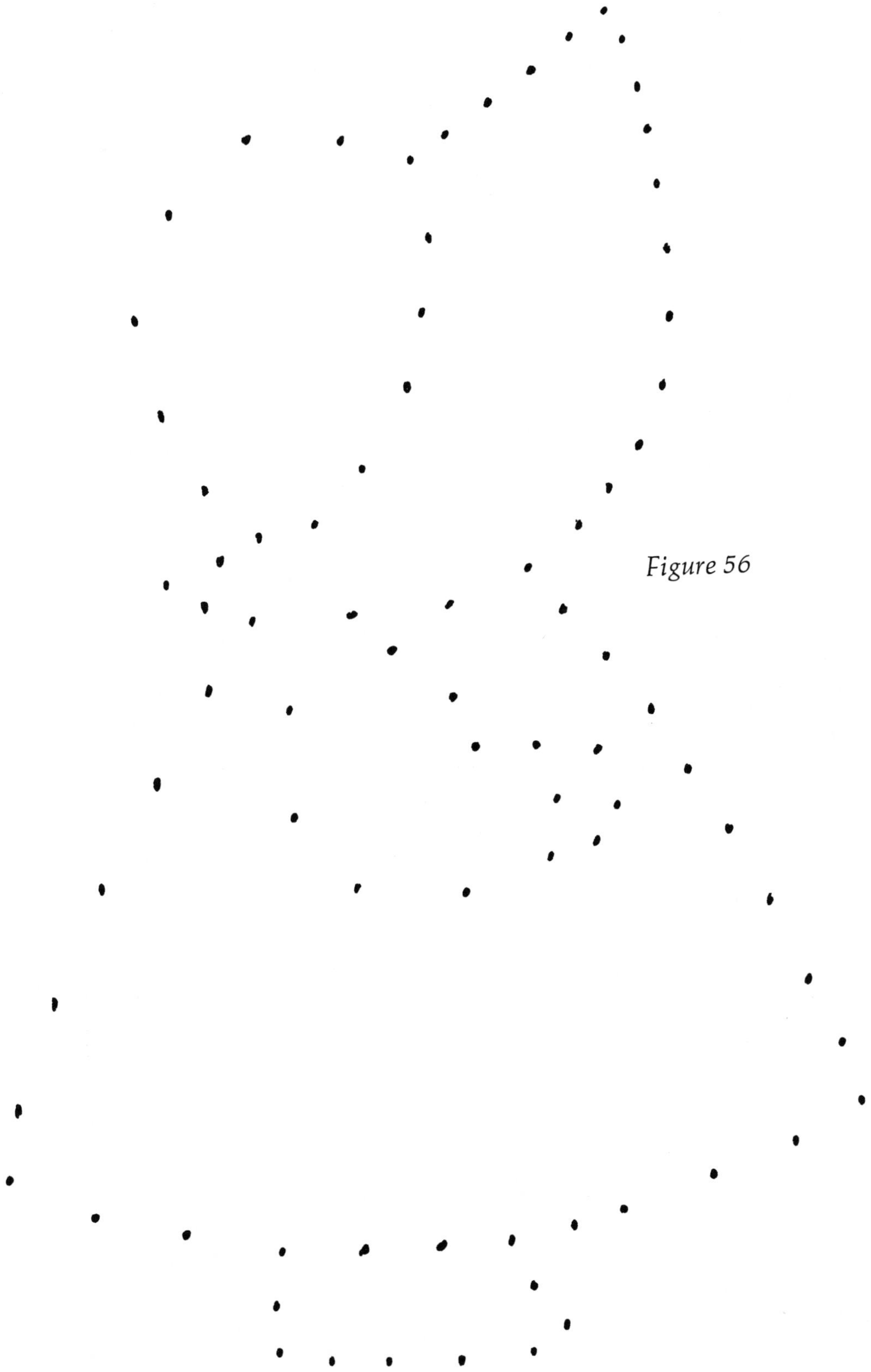

Figure 56

the shot-full-of-holes "Sunbonnet Sue" on the right side of the fabric and hold her down. Lightly twist a pencil in all the holes, making dots only dark enough to see.

"Sue" is then stacked: backing, batting, and the top square.

Baste from the center out to edges.

Dot to Dot

Starting at the centermost point quilt from dot to dot, being sure to go through the three layers. Don't end the thread unnecessarily; run it through the batting if you want to get to another section.

Appliquéd "Sue" and plain "Sue" look very well together in a quilt.

PATCHWORK AND PIECEWORK QUILTING DESIGNS

A square may be quilted with plain lines. These lines are called grids.

Grids are made by placing a ruler down on the right side of the fabric. Mark dots along the edge, flip the ruler over, and continue marking dots. Quilt from dot to dot and from the center out to within ½ inch of the edges (*Figures 57, 58, 59*).

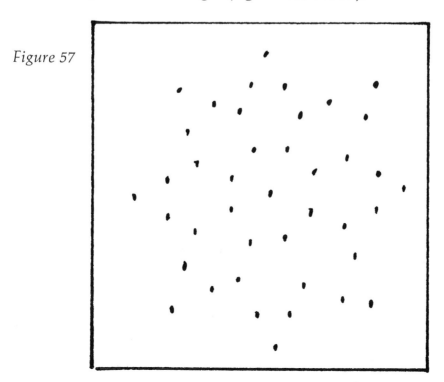

Figure 57

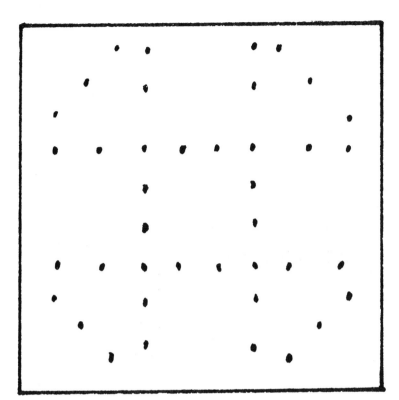

Figure 58

Figure 59

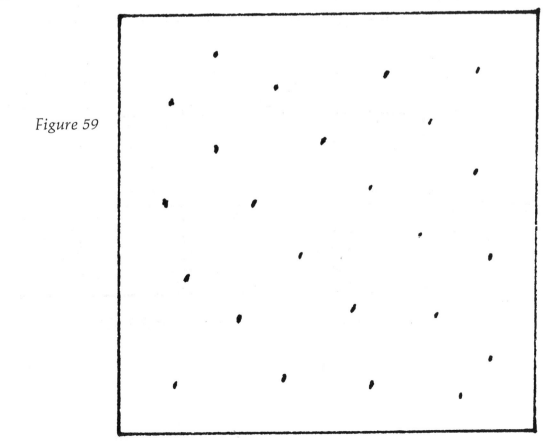

Figure 60

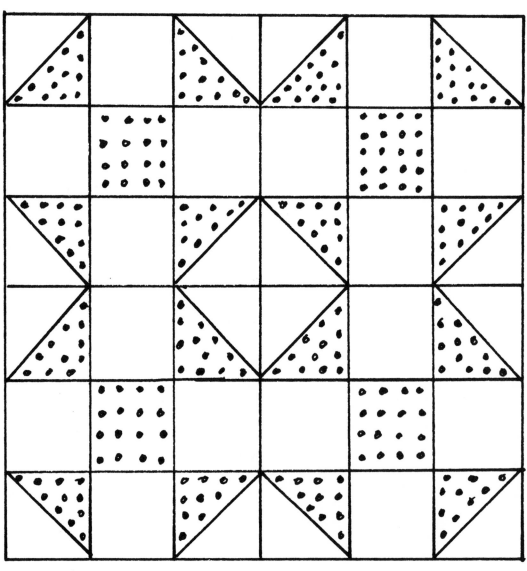

four squares joined together

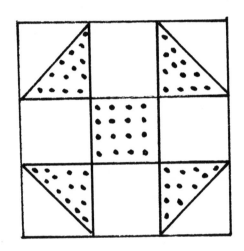

3
PIECEWORK

Have you ever marveled at "Log Cabin," "Babies' Blocks," "Monkey Wrench," "Bow Tie"? These old-time traditional patterns are made up of small pieces of fabric sewn together, and they may in turn make up another overall geometrical design (*Figure 60*). See Plate 19.

Figure 61 is made up of triangles and squares. Make two sets of cardboard patterns (templates). One set will include the ¼-inch seam allowance needed for sewing the pieces together. The other set will be the actual size of the pattern. With both sets the block will be accurate, which is most important in piecework!

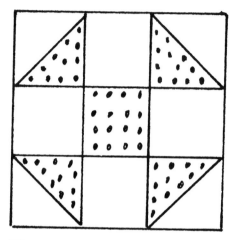

Figure 61

First make the actual-size set of templates. Using the corners and edges of a shirt cardboard, mark off two 4-inch squares (*Figure 62*). Cut out both squares; cut one in half, making two triangles (discard one). These are your actual-size templates: one square and one triangle.

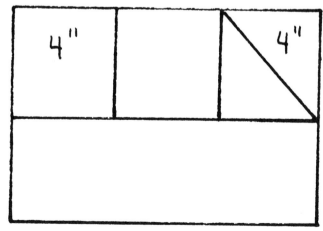

Figure 62

Now make the larger templates, which include the ¼-inch seam allowance needed for sewing the pieces together. Using the corners and edges of another shirt cardboard, mark off and cut one 4½-inch square on the left-hand side as in *Figure 63*. You now have one square 4½ inches x 4½ inches, which includes the ¼-inch seam allowance on all four sides. You can see this by placing the actual-size 4-inch square on top.

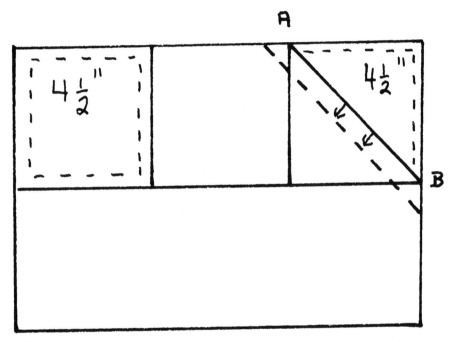

Figure 63

Draw a second 4½-inch square in the right-hand corner. Draw a straight line from *A* to *B* as in *Figure 63*, dividing the square into two triangles. The outside triangle already has the ¼-inch seam allowance on two edges. Take your ruler and add ¼ inch along line *A*–*B* indicated by the arrows. Cut on the broken line. You now have a 4½-inch triangle which includes the seam allowance on all three sides. You can see this by placing the 4-inch actual-size triangle on top.

Set the smaller set of templates aside. The *larger* ones are used for cutting the fabric.

PRINTS AND PLAINS—FOR SQUARES AND TRIANGLES

You will cut (*Figure 64*):

4 print triangles
4 plain triangles
1 print square
4 plain squares

If any of the fabrics are dark, a white dressmaker pencil is a must.

(*Text continues on page 81.*)

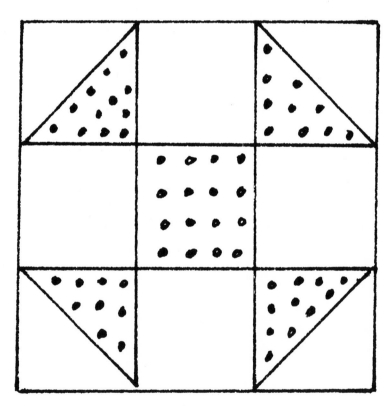

Figure 64

Plate 1.
Betty's patchwork star quilt for her antique bed—four top squares joined together on a large back square.

Plate 2.
Kappy's pieced quilt called "Connecticut"—four top squares joined together on a large back square.

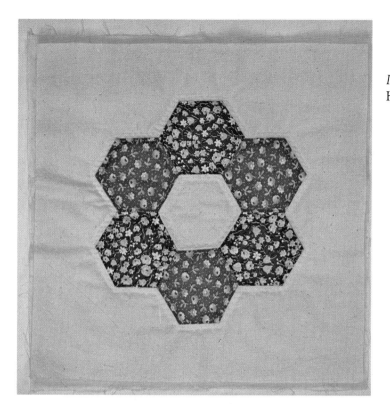

Plate 3.
Hexagon square—patchwork.

Plate 4.
Star—patchwork.

Plate 5.
Wallpaper flowers—
appliqué.

Plate 6.
"Sunbonnet Sue"—
appliqué.

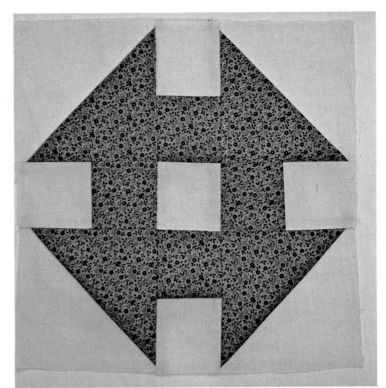

Plate 7.
Piecework.

Plate 8.
Wall-hanging sampler with "Farmer Frank."

Plate 9.
Tied quilt—names embroidered on a square by some of our students.

Plate 10.
"The Wrench"—piecework tied quilt for a bassinet by Betty.

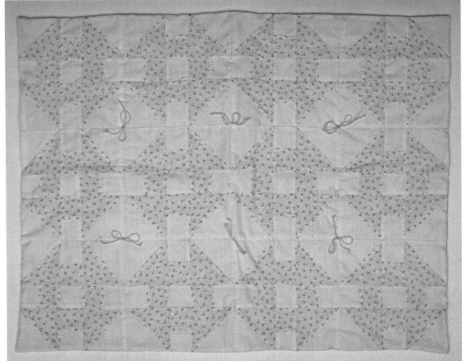

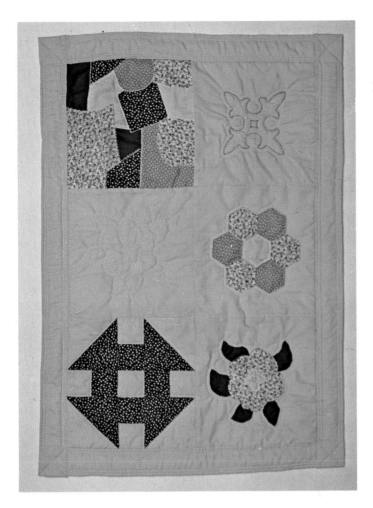

Plate 11.
The class sampler.

Plate 12.
Biscuits.

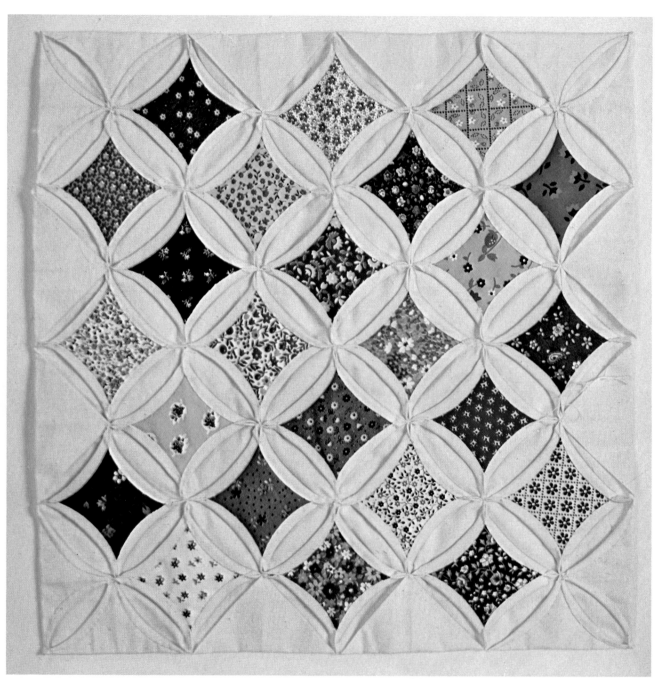

Plate 13.
"Cathedral Window."

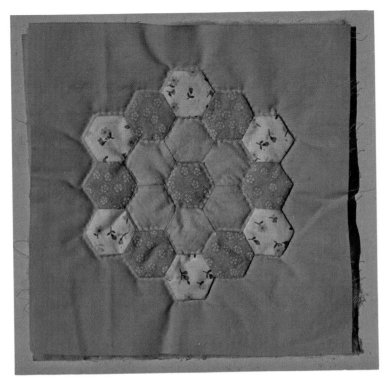

Plate 14.
"Grandmother's Flower
Garden."

Plate 15.
"Parade Hill Farm"—wall hang-
ing; a combination of piecework,
appliqué, and embroidery by
Kappy.

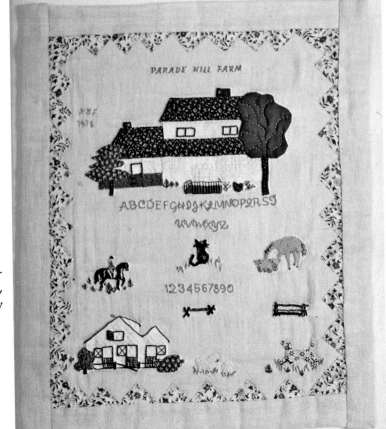

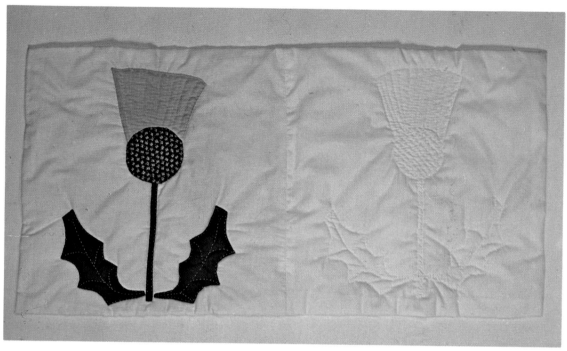

Plate 16.
Appliqué thistle and plain quilting.

Plate 17.
"Friendship" or "Dresden Plate" carriage quilt—patchwork.

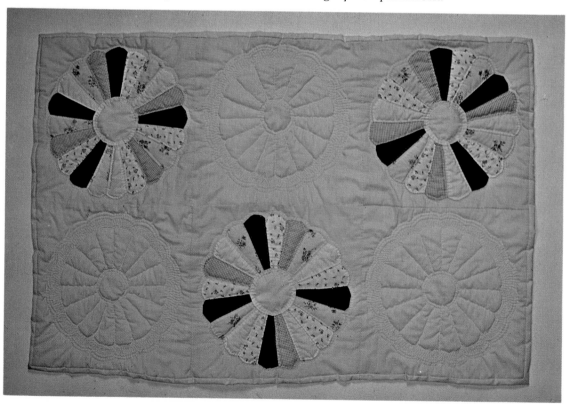

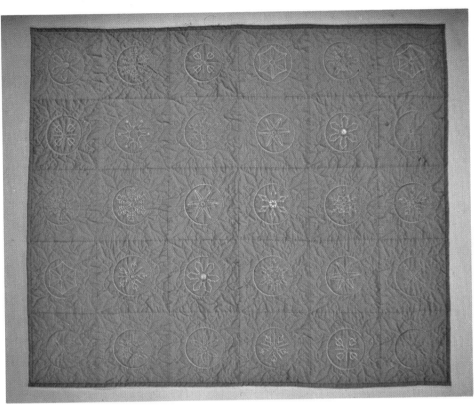

Plate 18.
Snowflake embroidered quilt by the authors and some of the members of New Canaan Sewing Group B.

Plate 19.
"Log Cabin"—a pieced quilt made for a sleigh bed by Kappy.

Plate 20.
"New Canaan Bicentennial" quilt—appliquéd scenes from our town; designed by Ann Price and made by the New Canaan Quilters.

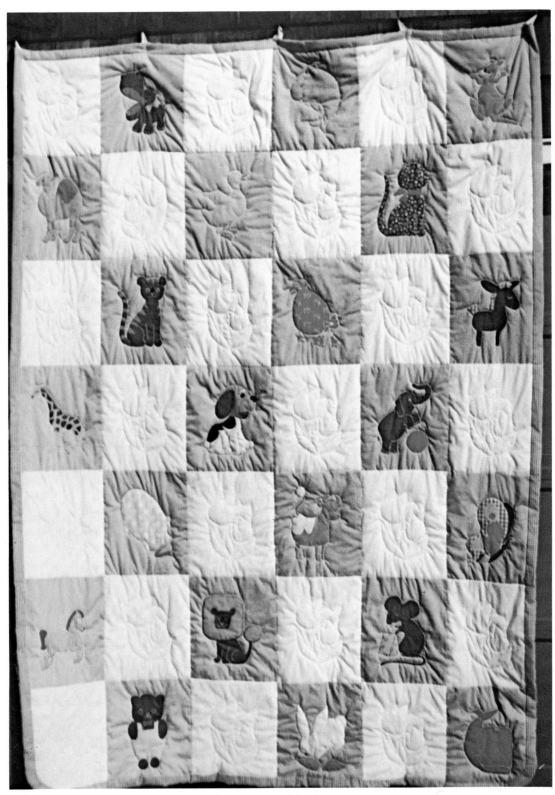

Plate 21.
Quilt for Sara by grandmother, Lois Harman (detail, Plate 22).

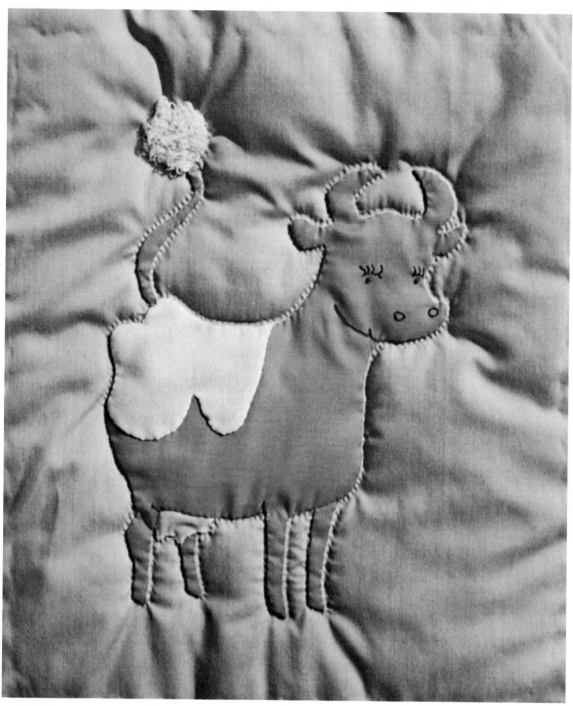

Plate 22.
Close-up of cow in Sara's quilt.

Plate 23.
Nancy Ryan's patch pieced pattern quilt.

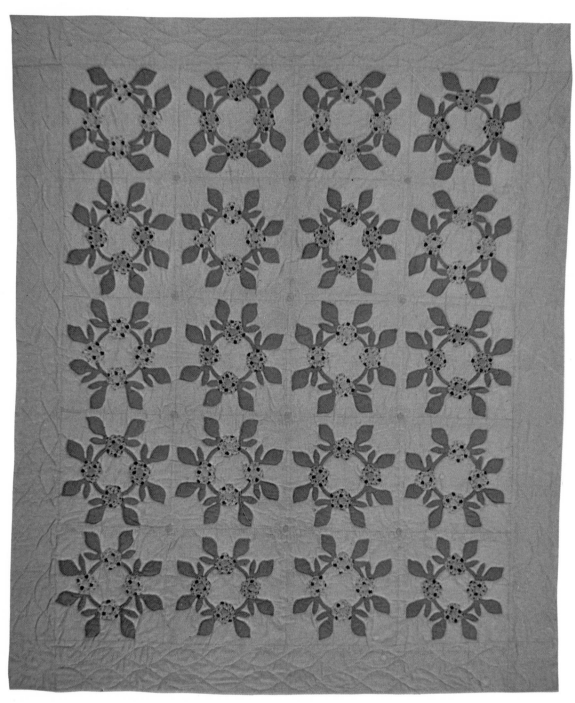

Plate 24.
"Wreath of Roses"—traditional appliqué pattern by the authors.

CUTTING UP

Place the 4½-inch square on the wrong side of the print fabric and mark around with a pencil. Place the 4½-inch triangle on the *wrong* side of the print fabric and draw around it. Flip it over, making another triangle. Use line *A–B* as the common line (*Figure 65*).

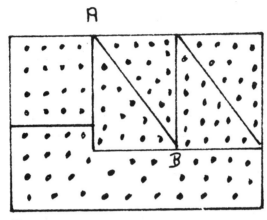

Figure 65

Place the 4½-inch square on the wrong side of the plain fabric, making four squares. Place the 4½-inch triangle on the *wrong* side of the plain fabric, making four triangles. Flip them over on common line *A–B* (*Figure 66*).

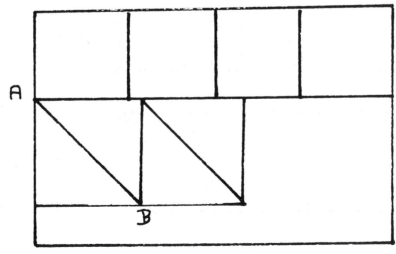

Figure 66

Using 4-inch actual-size templates make marks on the plain fabric *only*, as in *Figure 67*, to indicate the seam allowance. These marks are the guide lines for sewing.

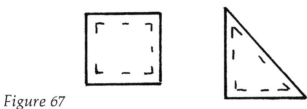

Figure 67

Cut out pieces on the solid lines and lay them in front of you, right side up, in their proper place (*Figure 68*).

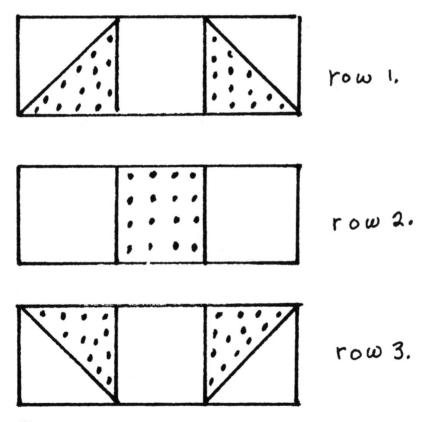

row 1.

row 2.

row 3.

Figure 68

Piecework is always sewn together by rows. Starting with row 1, first join plain and print triangles. You do this by placing right sides together. Pin and sew across the seam on guide lines, using single thread and a running stitch (*Figure 69*). Triangles should be pressed, placing seam allowance to one side—this makes a stronger seam (do not open the seam). Snip the fabric tails off (*Figure 70*).

Figure 69

running stitch

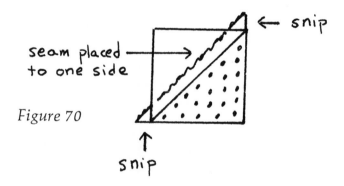

Figure 70

Sew the three parts of row 1 together. When you join the square to a triangle-made-square it will look like *Figure 71*. The distance between *A* and *B* is ¼ inch and will be taken up when you

Figure 71

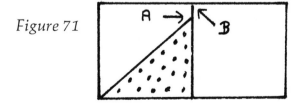

join the rows together. Sew the three parts of row 2, and the three parts of row 3, again pressing all the seams. Now match center seams and join row 1 to row 2, and then add row 3. Make all the seams as flat as possible. Press the finished square.

"QUILT IN"

The purpose of quilting is to hold the three layers together: the top, the batting, and the back (the back square is the underside of a quilt block, sometimes called the "backing" square). Stack, then baste the layers—the backing, batting, and top square—together like a sandwich. Baste the square with the knots on top for easy removal (*Figure 72*).

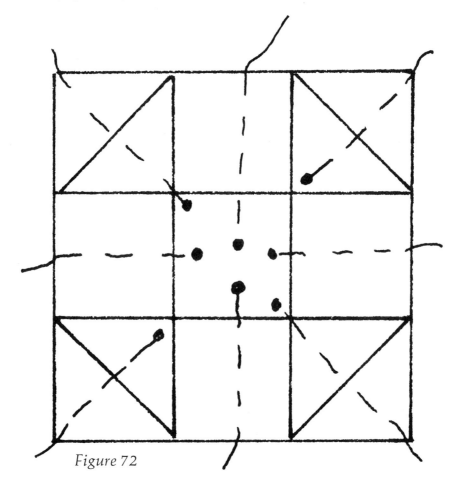

Figure 72

How to Quilt

The quilting stitch is a small running stitch going down through all three layers: the top, the batting, and the backing. It is evenly spaced and evenly stitched. Generally, you should have five to seven stitches to the inch, but don't worry if you don't—you should improve with practice (*Figures 73, 74*).

Figure 73

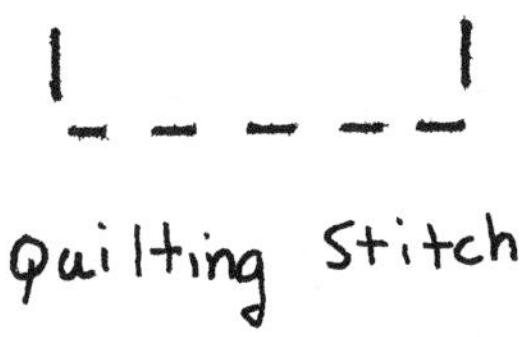

Quilting Stitch

Figure 74

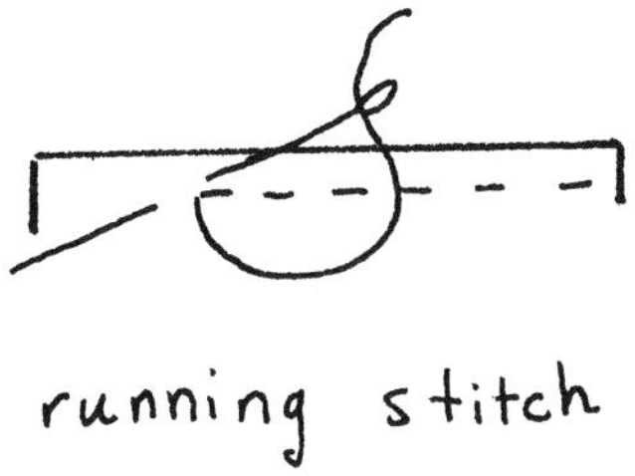

running stitch

Thread a needle with a single piece of quilting thread. Make a *small* knot, snip off the tail, and put your thimble on the third finger of your hand. Start by coming up from underneath at the center-most point (*Figure 75*). Give a quick pull, losing the knot in the batting—it makes a clicking sound. (This may take some practice. Pulling the backing square away makes it easier for the knot to slip through.) Go straight down through all three layers, touching your

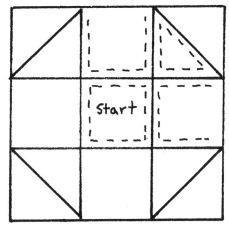

Figure 75

finger, and then come up to the top, making a small stitch. (Touching your finger ensures that you have gone through the three layers.) Take two, three, or four stitches on the needle and then draw through. If your finger gets sore wrap a piece of adhesive tape around it. This helps!

To end the thread off, go down to the underside of the backing square and take a stitch, going through the backing square and catching some batting. Then take another stitch right over the previous stitch. Now run the needle off to the side through the batting, pull the fabric up a little, and snip the thread off. The end is lost between the layers.

The amount of quilting you do is a matter of personal preference. It is most important to quilt from the center of the square toward the edges. This prevents the batting from bunching up in the center. Don't pull the stitches too tightly; let them flow. A very *important* point to remember: don't quilt any closer to the edge of the square than a good ½ inch. You will need the ½ inch of unquilted fabric when you join the square to another square in sewing the quilt together. (More than ½ inch unquilted fabric around the edge makes the whole process even easier!)

"Rome wasn't built in a day"—one square leads to another! Finish all the squares and turn to Chapter 4, "Building Blocks into Quilts," and put it together.

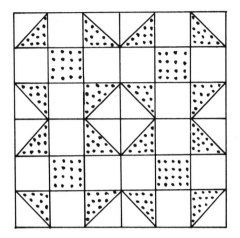

4
BUILDING BLOCKS
INTO QUILTS

The squares are finished—
hurray, you did it!

Join all the squares together.

Lay the squares on the floor in their proper place. Sew all of row 1 together as follows (*Figure 76*): Starting with squares 1 and 2, place right sides together and sew a seam joining just the tops, not the batting or backing. Use a running stitch or sewing machine and

Figure 76

allow at least ¼-inch seam allowance. Sew all the squares together in each row, and then lay each row down on the floor in proper order (*Figure 77*).

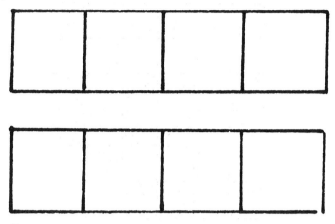

Figure 77

Working with each row *wrong* side up:

1. Place seam allowance (the top square seams you have just sewn) to one side—do not open seam.

2. Place batting from one side over the seam.

3. Trim batting from the other side so it abuts.

4. Lay backing from one side over batting, trimming when necessary.

5. The backing from the other side is turned under ¼ inch and placed over the previous seam. This seam is folded and pinned in the same direction on all the blocks. Do not sew yet—only pin (*Figure 78*)!

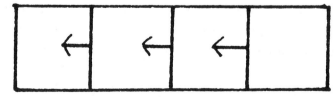

Figure 78

THE END IS IN SIGHT—JOIN THE ROWS

Starting with the first row: Right sides together, match the center seams, pinning and stitching just the tops, not the batting or the backing. Use a running stitch or machine and allow at least ¼-inch seam allowance. Continue joining all the horizontal rows in this manner (*Figure 79*).

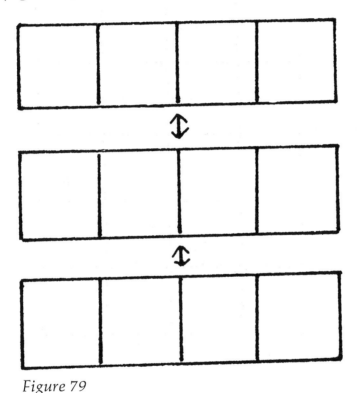

Figure 79

Turn the quilt over so the back is facing up. The vertical rows are neatly pinned. Begin with the first horizontal row and place the seam allowance (of the seams you have just sewn) to one side. Do not open the seams. Place the batting from one side over the seam, and trim the batting from the other side as it abuts. Then lay the backing over the batting and trim when necessary. Adjust all the vertical seams so they match up with all the other vertical seams in all the rows.

The mystery of the extra ½-inch larger back square unravels: you need it to help all the seams match up.

All the vertical seams are facing in the same direction. Now pin the horizontal seams in the same direction (*Figure 80*).

Blind stitch all the back seams of the quilt.

Hang in there—the quilt is almost finished. All it needs is framing. Now on to the edges.

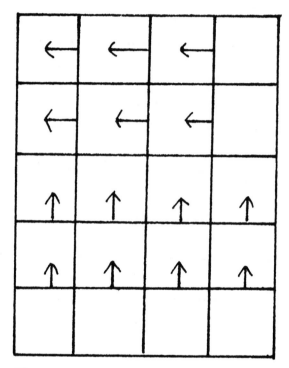

Figure 80

STRIPS AND BORDERS

Trim all four edges of your quilt so they are even. Strips and borders are attached to the quilt in the same manner. Strips are narrow and do not need batting. Borders are wide and therefore must have batting and should be quilted.

Strips

First, pin the *width* strips, right sides together, to the top and bottom of the quilt. Stitch by hand or machine through all thick-

nesses. Fold the strips over the ends of the quilt and turn the raw
edge under ¼ inch. Blind stitch to the quilt back, being sure to cover
the previous seam. Trim the excess strip even with the sides of the
quilt (*Figure 81*).

Figure 81

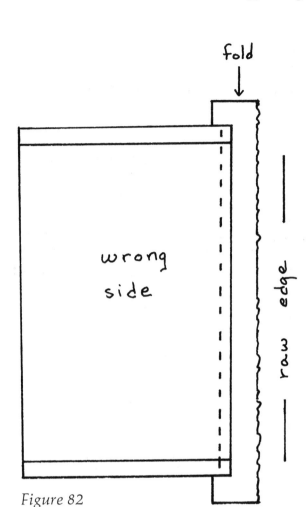

Figure 82

With right sides together, pin the *length* strips to both sides of the quilt, allowing the extra inches to hang over both ends. Stitch by hand or machine through all thicknesses. Turn the quilt over, fold the extra inches to the back, and pin (*Figure 82*). Turn the outside raw edge under ¼ inch, fold the strip over, and blind stitch to the quilt back, covering the previous seam.

Borders

Fold borders in half lengthwise and press, making a sharp crease. Cut the batting as follows: Take one width border and cut a piece of batting the same size. Now cut the batting in half length-wise, making the two pieces needed for the top and bottom borders. Cut the batting for the *length* the same way but make it longer to include the width of the finished top and bottom borders.

Pin the width borders on both ends of the quilt, right sides together. Stitch by hand or machine through all thicknesses. Turn the quilt over so that the wrong side of the quilt and borders are facing up. Lay the batting between the quilt edge and the crease (*Figure 83*). Fold the border over the batting so the crease becomes the outside edge of the quilt. Turn the raw edge under, being sure that your seam is covered, and pin carefully. Baste the border across its width to secure the batting *before* you blind stitch it down to the back of the quilt.

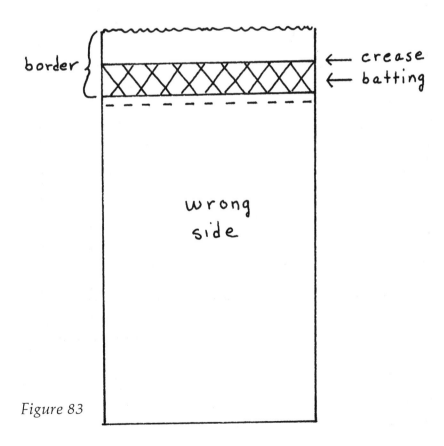

Figure 83

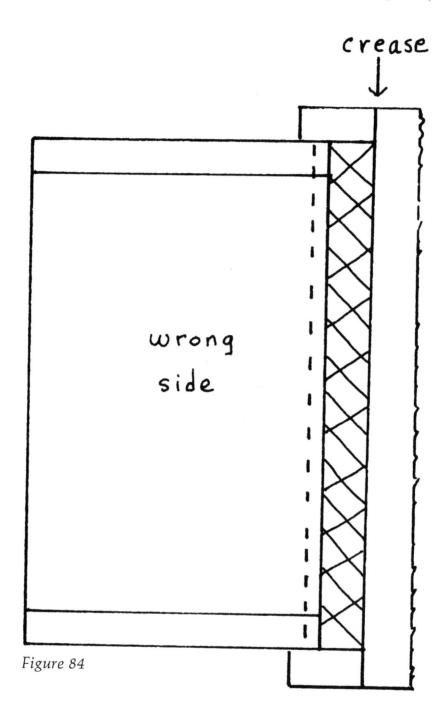

Figure 84

Pin the length borders on the quilt with right sides together, allowing the extra inches to hang over the finished top and bottom borders. Stitch by hand or machine through all thicknesses. Turn the quilt over so that the wrong side of the quilt and border is facing up. Lay the batting between the quilt edge and the crease, trimming if necessary (*Figure 84*).

Fold the border over the batting so the crease becomes the outside edge of the quilt. Turn the raw edge under, being sure that your seam is covered, and pin carefully. Baste the border across the width to secure the batting *before* you blind stitch it down to the back of the quilt.

FAMILY REJOICES

The heirloom quilt is finished. Beds will now be made, laundry will be done, and dinner will be on time! Proudly embroider your name and date on the back.

YOU HAVE MADE A QUILT!

See Plate 21.

5
FURTHER FUN

TIE ONE ON

A tied quilt is a quick quilt and a confidence-builder. It is made by joining all the top squares together, making the whole quilt top in one piece (*Figure 85*). The batting and the backing are each bought in one large piece. A sheet could be used for the backing. Batting can be bought in all sizes except king size. When making a king-size tied

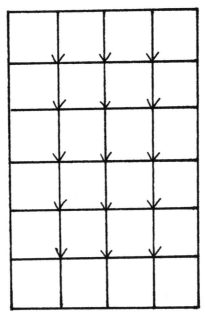

Figure 85

Tied Quilt

quilt buy two packages of single-bed size and join them together with long basting stitches (*Figure 86*). See Plate 9.

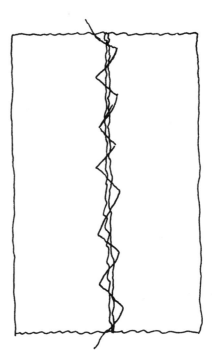

Figure 86

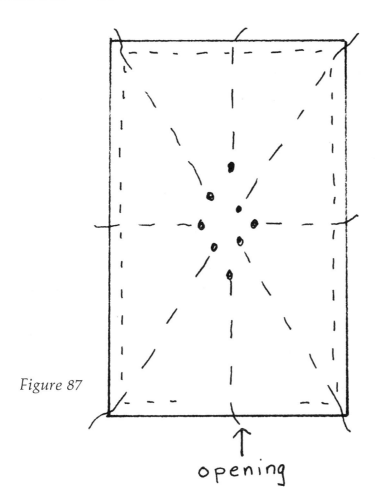

Figure 87

opening

Place the tied quilt on the floor in the following order:

1. The batting.

2. The backing with the *right* side facing up.

3. The quilt top with the *wrong* side facing up.

Pin and baste the layers together, working from the center out to the edges. Stitch on the machine (or by hand) around the edges, being sure to catch all three layers (*Figure 87*). Leave one end open for turning. Trim the edges even if necessary. Turn the quilt inside out and blind stitch the opening closed.

Tie It

Place the quilt on the floor with the side you want the knots to be on facing up. Mark with pins where knots will go (*Figure 88*). Thread a needle with yarn. Go down through the three layers, take a ¼-inch stitch on the underneath side, and come back up to the top. Make a square knot. (For the benefit of the non-yachting sewer here's how: right over left tie, and then left over right tie.) Snip the ends off to the length you want.

CRAZY THINGS WITH "CRAZY PATCH"

Cut a 12-inch square of muslin. Start at one corner and pin scraps of different colors and prints on top of the muslin base. Overlap them as you pin. Arrange and rearrange—do your thing. Turn the edges under ¼ inch and blind stitch down. On the underneath

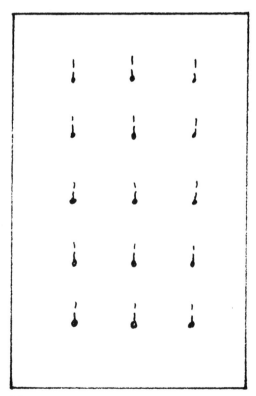

Figure 88

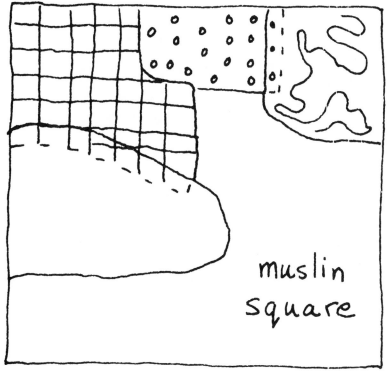

muslin
square

Figure 89

pieces leave the raw edges flat when possible. Cut away excess material to reduce the bulk (*Figure 89*).

"Crazy Patch" can be made on the sewing machine, using the zigzag stitch. Raw edges are left lying flat and are zigzagged over.

Press the square when it is completed.

The seams may be covered with embroidery stitches. This adds to the beauty of a crazy quilt.

Don't quilt "Crazy Patch." There are too many thicknesses, so tie it. One way to tie it is to have the ties show only on the back because very often the top is busy enough. Starting at the center of the square, bring the ties from the back up toward the top, but catch only the muslin base. Then go down through the back and make a square knot. It is a little easier, however, to come all the way through to the top, make a small stitch, and go back down with a square knot on the back.

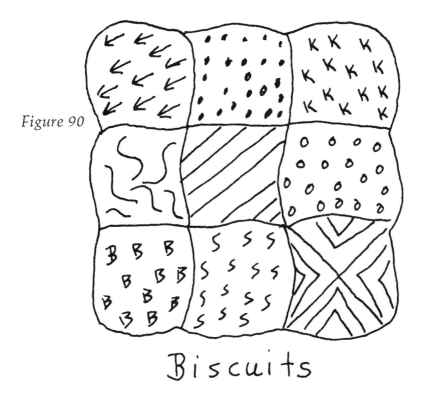

Figure 90

Biscuits

BISCUITS

Biscuits are puffy squares filled with pillow stuffing instead of batting. They are whipped together to make a quilt (*Figure 90*). Biscuits may be any size. The top square is always 1½ inches larger than the bottom square. See Plate 12.

Cut two cardboard patterns, one large and one small. Use the large pattern on one fabric and the small on another. (The small pattern is for the bottom and the larger one for the top.)

Right sides together, pin at the corners one large square and one small square (*Figure 91*). Then pin a pleat on each side of all the corners. The pleats face the center (*Figure 92*). Stitch a ¼-inch seam around. Leave an opening on one side for turning inside out (*Figure 93*).

Turn inside out and stuff with pillow stuffing. Blind stitch the opening closed.

Make another biscuit. Join the two by placing the bottom sides together and whipping across the edge. This seam will not show.

Young people, especially boys, seem to love this type of quilt.

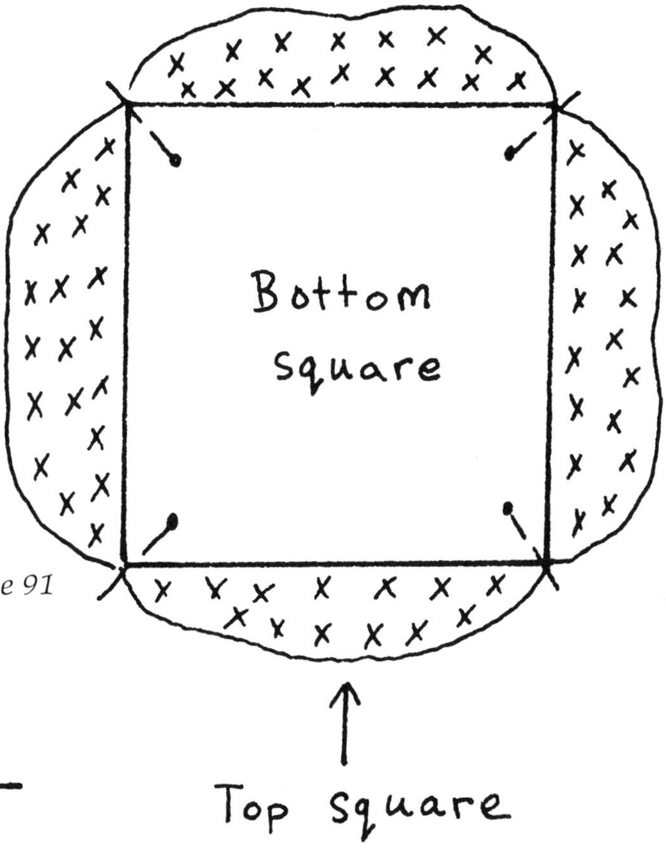

Bottom square

Top square

Figure 91

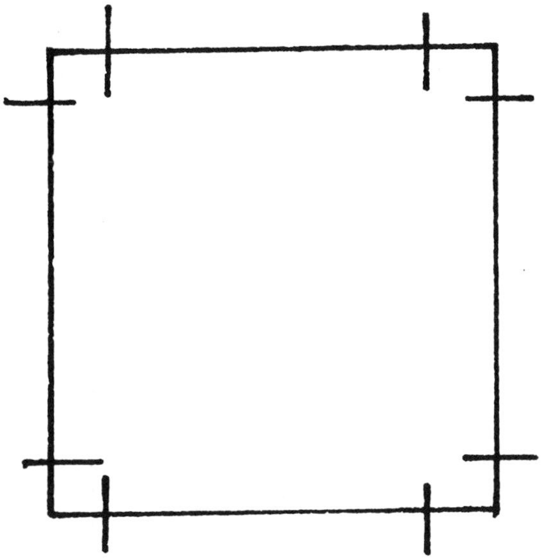

Figure 92

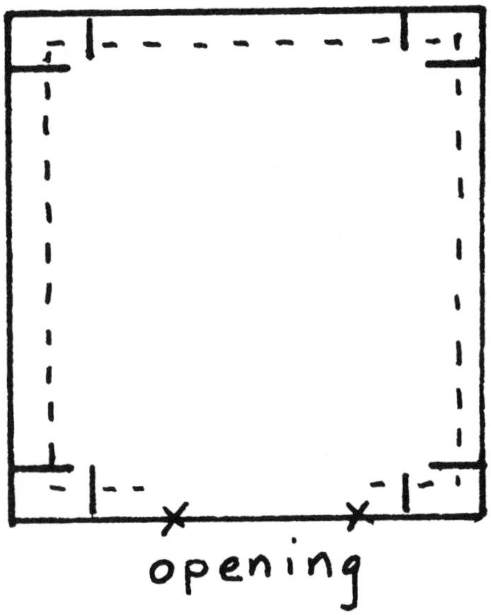

Figure 93

opening

"CATHEDRAL WINDOW"

"Cathedral Window" is very impressive and makes a lovely pillow or a beautiful coverlet. It is never quilted. When the fabric is sewn together the square is finished! See Plate 13.

Cut two accurate 9-inch squares of plain fabric. With right sides *inside*, fold each square in half and stitch a ¼-inch seam on each end (*Figure 94*). This sewing may be done by hand or machine.

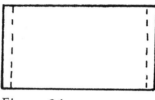

Figure 94

One at a time, make a square by matching center seams of line A–B (*Figure 95*). Sew by hand or machine seam C–D, leaving an opening for turning (*Figure 96*).

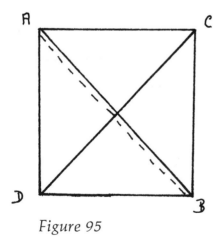

Figure 95

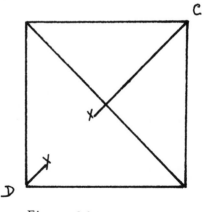

Figure 96

Turn each square right side out, poking the corners with a pencil so they are sharp. Blind stitch the opening closed. Press.

Place each square in front of you with the seam side down. Using a double thread, place the needle through the tip of point *A* in *Figure 97*. Don't worry about the knot on top showing. Then pick up point *B* the same way, drawing both together so the points touch each other, meeting at the center (*Figure 98*). Put the needle through

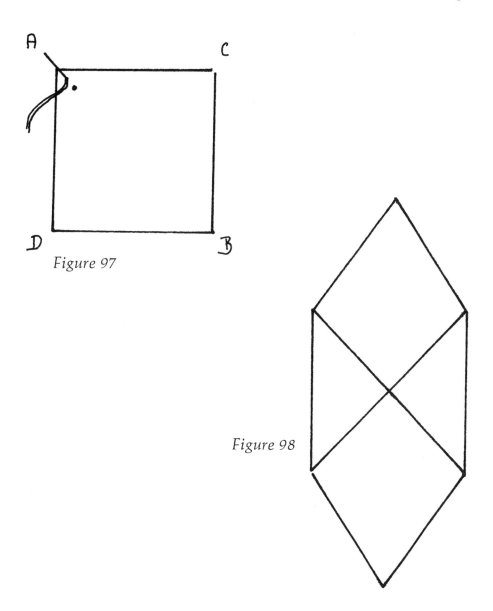

Figure 97

Figure 98

to the underside at the intersection, come back up to the top, and pick up points *C* and *D* as you did *A* and *B*. Go down through the intersection again and then come back up and knot the thread off. Press. The two squares will look like *Figures 99* and *100*.

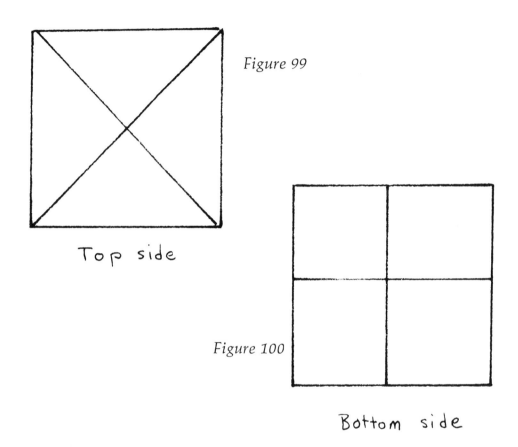

Figure 99

Top side

Figure 100

Bottom side

Join the two squares by placing the bottom sides together, matching the center seam, and whipping across the edge. This is the seam you will cover with a print fabric to make the "window" (*Figure 101*).

Cut a small print square ¼ inch *smaller* than the area you are covering. Pin it on top of the seam. Start in the middle of one side, turn the folded edge over the print fabric, and blind stitch it down. Sew all four sides (*Figure 102*).

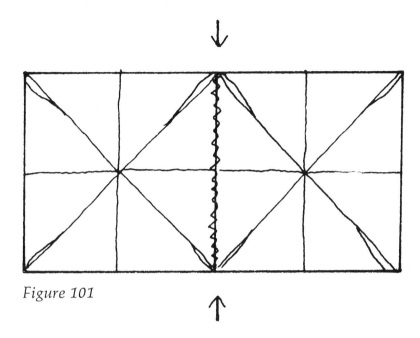

Figure 101

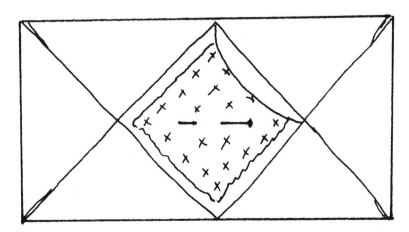

Figure 102

You need nine squares to make a pillow. Each row is made up of three squares. You must complete each row first and then whip the rows together. You will see that in joining the rows you will create a seam that must be covered with print fabric (*Figure 103*).

You may want to fold back the folds on the outside sections and blind stitch them down (line *A–B* in the figure). This gives the top a finished look and makes a pattern of the folded edges. A little piece of pillow stuffing can also be put under the small print fabric. This gives an added puffy look.

When you make a "Cathedral Window" pillow the cording is placed on the pillow back. The "Cathedral Window" top is then sewn on by hand.

You may join many blocks together (by rows—important!) to make a lovely coverlet.

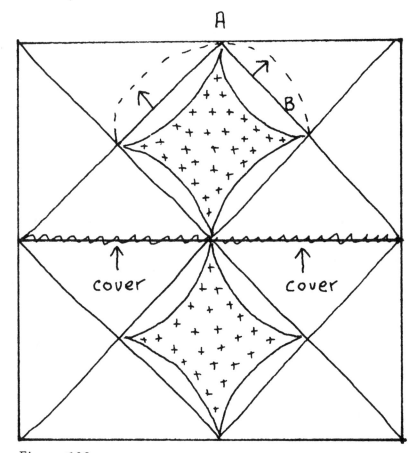

Figure 103

"GRANDMOTHER'S FLOWER GARDEN" PILLOW

Use two or three print fabrics and a plain color. The plain color is the path" running through "Grandmother's Garden." See Plate 14.

Make fabric hexagons, using the hexagon pattern (*Figure 104*). Then whip them together, following *Figure 105*:

1. Whip all the hexagons in each row together.

2. Then join the rows, fitting each hexagon into place. You will be sewing one side of the hexagon at a time, zigzagging as you sew.

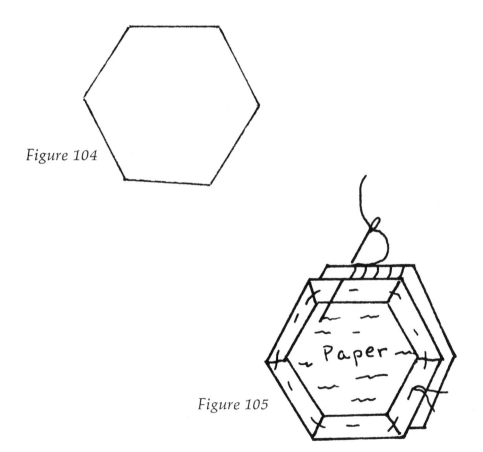

Figure 104

Figure 105

Press the hexagon flower and then remove the papers. Blind stitch it onto a background square. Press again and get it ready for quilting. Quilt it, stuff it, and present it to "Grandpa."

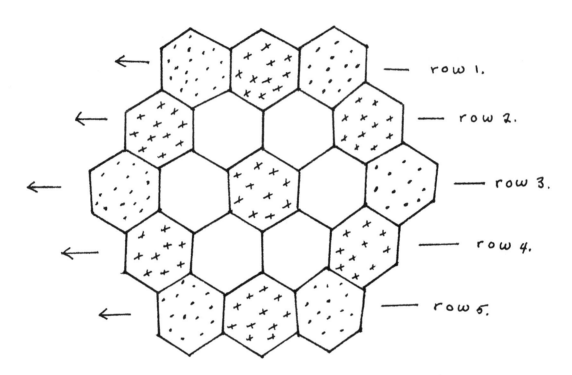

Figure 106

ADDITIONAL
QUILT
PATTERNS

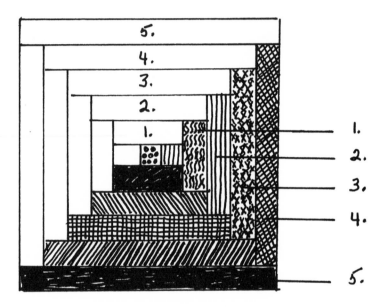

Log Cabin

See Plate 19.

LOG CABIN

This variation is called "Barn Raising."

Each square has a dark and a light side. Cut three center pieces 1½ inches by 1½ inches. All the rest of the strips are 1½ inches by:

1 = 3½ inches
2 = 5½ inches
3 = 7½ inches
4 = 9½ inches
5 = 11½ inches

Cut two lights and two darks of each size for one square with the exception of number 5, which has only one dark and one light.

First sew the three small center pieces together, then:
add number 1 light strip to the top
add number 1 dark strip to the bottom
add number 1 light strip to the side
add number 1 dark strip to the other side

Continue adding:
number 2 light strip to the top
number 2 dark strip to the bottom
number 2 light strip to the light side
number 2 dark strip to the dark side

It is very important to add the strips in this order. The last row has only one dark and one light strip. The seam allowance taken should be ¼ inch. It is included in the pattern. This square will measure approximately 11 inches.

WREATH OF ROSES APPLIQUÉ

The circle for the wreath is made from a bias strip. It is sewn in place first on a background square. The flowers and leaves are then placed on top and blind stitched down.

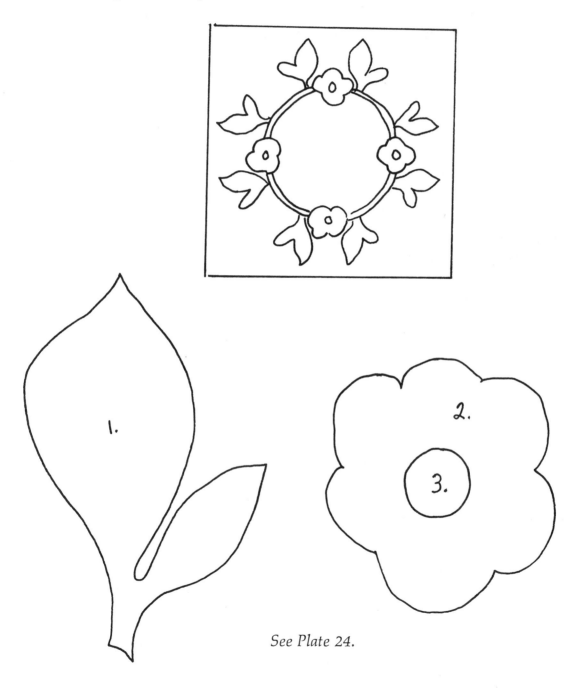

See Plate 24.

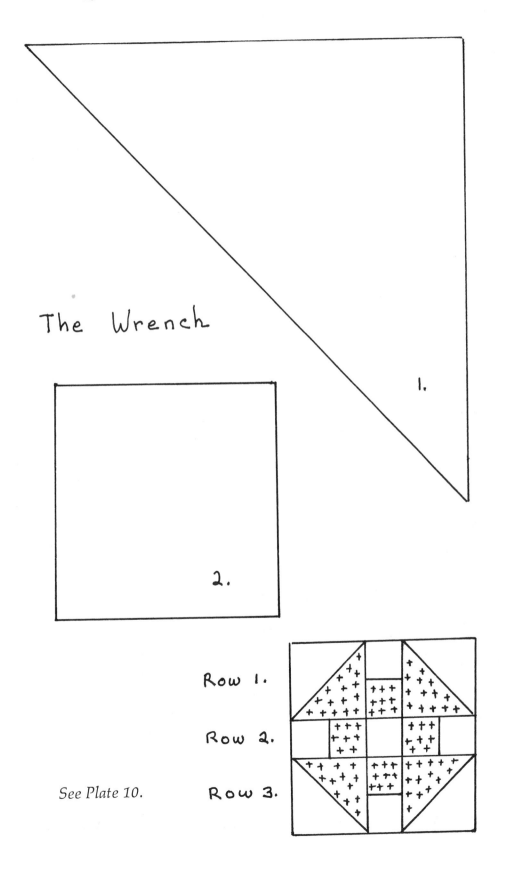

The Wrench

1.

2.

Row 1.

Row 2.

See Plate 10.   Row 3.

See Plate 21.

1.

2.

3.

Hen and Chicks Appliqué with Embroidery

1.

2.

3.

See Plate 16.

Appliqué and Quilting

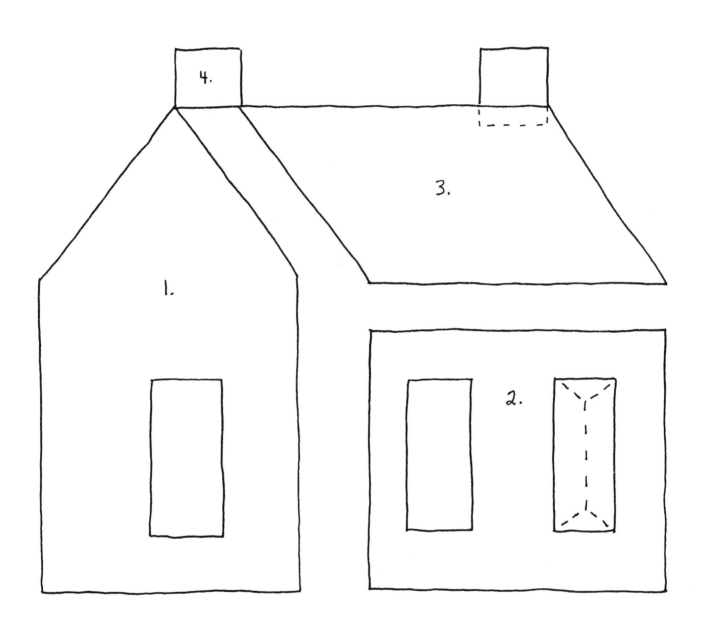

School House Appliqué

SCHOOL HOUSE APPLIQUÉ

Cut each section from colorful calico and appliqué the pieces in place on a background square.

Slit the windows as shown by the broken lines, fold the edges under, and blind stitch down. Add embroidery for the shutters.

You will need to add a ¼-inch seam allowance to each section.

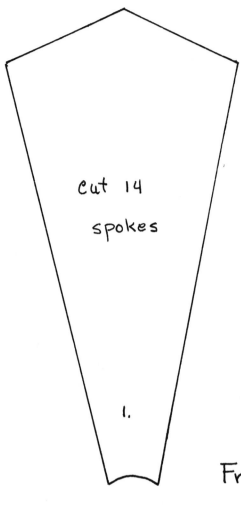

cut 14

spokes

1.

Friendship "Wheel"

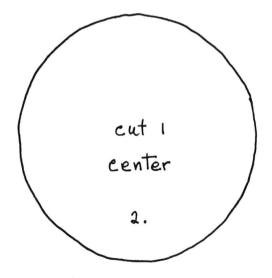

cut 1

center

2.

See Plate 17.

THE FRIENDSHIP "WHEEL"

Its proper name is "Friendship Ring" or "Dresden Plate."

The pattern is given without the seam allowance, but the best way to make it up is to include the seam allowance in the pattern. Work with two patterns as you do in piecework, two with the seam allowance and one without.

Seam the spokes together. Press and blind stitch down on a 14-inch background square. Appliqué the center on top.

1.

2.

3.

Cardinal Appliqué with Embroidery

A B C D E F
G H I J K L M
N O P Q R S T U
V W X Y Z

a b c d e f
g h i j k l m
n o p q r s t u
v w x y z

1 2 3 4 5 6 7 8 9 0

Barbara
November 28, 1955

Fold

Plain Quilting

Embroidered
Name and Date

Terms Used in Quilt-making

Appliqué—A free-form pattern "laid" on a top square.

Backing square—Underside of the quilt block.

Batting—The filler inside the quilt.

Block—One square in a quilt.

Patchwork—A combination of piecework and appliqué—for example, the piecing of geometrical shapes, appliquéd on a top square.

Piecework—Geometrical-shape pieces of fabric sewn together to make up a design.

Quilt—A bed covering made up of two pieces of cloth with a filler in between. Stitched designs hold the layers together. This is called quilting.

Selvage—An edge of a woven fabric, so formed as to prevent raveling.

Setting—The arrangement of all the squares, or blocks, in a quilt.

Straight of goods—There are two straights: one follows the vertical selvage and the other is at right angles to it (across the width of the fabric).

Template—A pattern used in quilt-making.

Top square—Top face of the quilt block.

Bibliography

BOGEN, CONSTANCE. *A Beginners' Book of Patchwork, Appliqué and Quilting.* New York: Dodd, Mead and Company, 1974.

FRAGER, DOROTHY. *The Quilting Primer.* Radnor, Pennsylvania: Chilton Book Company, 1974.

HEARD, AUDREY, AND PRYOR, BEVERLY. *Complete Guide to Quilting.* Des Moines, Iowa: Meredith Corp./Better Homes and Gardens, 1974.

LEHMAN, BONNIE. *Quick and Easy Quilting.* New York: Hearthside Press, 1972.

MAHLER, CELINE BLANCHARD. *Once Upon a Quilt.* New York: Van Nostrand Reinhold Co., 1973.

WILSON, ERICA. *Crewel Embroidery.* New York: Charles Scribner's Sons, 1962.